Case Interview Math, Math, Math

Master Case Math in Days, Not Months

Taylor Warfield

All rights reserved. No part of this book may be reproduced, distributed, or transmitted in any form by any means, including electronic, mechanical, photocopy, recording, or otherwise, without the prior written permission of the author.

This book and the information contained in this book are for informative purposes only. The information in this book is distributed on an as-is basis, without warranty. The author makes no legal claims and the material is not meant to substitute legal or financial counsel.

The author, publisher, and copyright holder assume no responsibility for the loss or damage caused or allegedly caused, directly or indirectly, by the use of information contained in this book. The author and publisher specifically disclaim any liability incurred from the use or application of the contents of this book.

Throughout this book, trademarked names are referenced. Rather than using a trademark symbol for every occurrence of a trademarked name, we state that we are using the names in an editorial fashion only and to the benefit of the trademark owner, with no intention of infringement of the trademark.

This book contains several fictitious examples that involve names of real people, places, and organizations. Any slights of people, places, or organizations are unintentional.

Copyright © 2025 by Taylor Warfield
All rights reserved

ISBN-13: 978-1-7333381-4-1

Table of Contents

1. Introduction 1
2. Arithmetic 7
3. Fractions 17
4. Decimals 27
5. Percentages 35
6. Ratios and Proportions 45
7. Statistics 55
8. Algebra 73
9. Profit Formulas 85
10. Investment Formulas 101
11. Operations Formulas 109
12. Market Share Formulas 119
13. Finance Formulas 127
14. Charts and Graphs 139
15. Market Sizing 153
16. Mental Math Strategies 169
17. Case Math Strategies 187
18. Practice Problems 193
19. Next Steps 269
20. About the Author 273

1. Introduction

Why Case Interviews Matter

A case interview, also known as a "case" for short, is a 30- to 45-minute exercise in which you and the interviewer work together to develop a recommendation or answer to a business problem.

You'll be presented with a business problem and asked to analyze the situation, structure your thinking, and propose a solution, often involving quantitative analysis, creativity, and business judgement.

These business problems can be anything that real companies face:

- How can Amazon increase its profitability?
- What can Apple do to increase customer retention?
- How should Nike price its newest shoe?
- Where should Disney open another Disneyland theme park?

Every major consulting firm uses case interviews in their interview process to evaluate candidates.

This includes firms such as McKinsey, BCG, Bain, Deloitte, Oliver Wyman, LEK, Kearney, Strategy&, EY-Parthenon, and Roland Berger.

Whether you're applying for a generalist consulting role or a more specialized track, expect to face several rounds of case interviews during the recruiting process.

Why do nearly all consulting firms rely so heavily on case interviews?

The answer: because they test the exact skills consultants use on the job every day.

A strong performance in a case interview shows that you can:

- Break down complex problems into manageable parts
- Think logically under pressure
- Perform quick, accurate math
- Communicate clearly and confidently
- Interpret data and make decisions based on evidence
- Demonstrate business intuition

Case interviews are designed to predict your future success as a consultant.

If you enjoy tackling cases, chances are you'll also enjoy consulting. If you struggle to structure your thoughts or perform basic case math, those weaknesses will likely carry over into real consulting projects.

This is why doing well in case interviews is critical. You will not land a consulting job offer unless you nail every single one of your case interviews.

Why Case Interview Math Matters

Nearly every case interview involves math. Whether you're estimating market size, calculating breakeven points, or analyzing a company's profit margins, you will deal with numbers in your cases.

In fact, math is one of the few constants across all types of case interviews. No matter what the industry, function, or case style is, expect to do math.

Case interview math is a fundamental part of what consultants do.

Clients hire consulting firms to solve tough business problems, many of which require data-driven solutions. You'll be expected to work with numbers regularly, whether it's building financial models, interpreting charts, or analyzing data sets.

Case interview math is a real-time check on your quantitative skills. It's the only opportunity interviewers have to directly observe how you approach quantitative problems under pressure.

Interviewers want to see if you can:

- Interpret quantitative information correctly

- Perform basic calculations accurately under pressure

- Avoid careless mistakes and double-check your work

- Explain your reasoning clearly and logically

Why Is Case Interview Math Hard

If case interview math feels difficult, you're not alone. Most candidates, even those from top schools or technical backgrounds, struggle with case math at first.

Why is case interview math so hard? There are several potential reasons.

First, you probably haven't done math in a while. In school and in most jobs, we rely heavily on calculators, spreadsheets, and software to do the heavy lifting.

In a case interview, you're expected to do calculations with pen and paper, without any digital tools.

Second, you're likely out of practice. Even if you used to be quick with numbers, math is like a muscle. If you haven't exercised it recently, it's going to feel slow and weak.

Third, there are specific formulas and concepts that show up in case interviews that you may not use in your daily life. These include things such as breakeven analysis, determining ROI, and calculating contribution margins.

If you've never had to calculate a weighted average or a market share by hand, these questions can catch you off guard.

Finally, case interview math is a bit like taking a math exam. You need to solve problems quickly while under pressure. The high stakes of an interview make doing math even more challenging.

However, I do have good news for you!

Case interview math is not inherently complicated. In fact, most case interview math is basic arithmetic. You'll never need to do any math that an intelligent middle school student couldn't figure out.

You don't need to know any calculus, trigonometry, linear algebra, or differential equations.

Like preparing for an exam, case interview math is a skill you can learn and improve with the right guidance and practice. I can confidently say that everyone is capable of mastering case math.

Who am I?

So, why should you bother learning from me and listening to my advice?

I'm Taylor Warfield, a former Bain Manager, interviewer, and founder of HackingTheCaseInterview.com. I've published a few best-selling books that have sold 50k+ copies worldwide:

- Hacking the Case Interview
- The Ultimate Case Interview Workbook
- Hacking the PM Interview

My YouTube channel, @HackingTheCaseInterview, has millions of views.

Through my books, online courses, and coaching, I've helped thousands of students and working professionals land offers in consulting.

So, you can be confident that you'll be getting the very best case interview math strategies and guidance in this book.

How to Best Use This Book

This book is designed to help you build the math skills you need to ace your case interviews as quickly and efficiently as possible. It's structured in three key sections:

1. **Math fundamentals**: The core concepts, formulas, and calculations that show up again and again in case interviews

2. **Practice problems**: Targeted exercises that reinforce the math fundamentals you've learned

3. **Math strategies**: Techniques for improving speed, accuracy, and confidence when doing case math

How to best use this book depends on how much time you have and what your current skill level is.

If you're short on time, skip straight to the math concepts you struggle with the most. Learn the fundamentals, review the examples, and complete the practice problems at the end of those chapters.

If you have more time, we recommend going through the book from start to finish. Even if some concepts feel familiar, the review can sharpen your skills and boost your confidence.

You may also learn something new that will save you time or prevent you from making a mistake during your interviews.

Whether you're brand new to case interviews or just need to brush up on your math, this book will provide you with everything you need to learn, practice, and master case interview math.

Let's get started!

2. Arithmetic

Why Arithmetic Matters

You may think that arithmetic is something too basic to worry about, but in case interviews, simple math errors can quickly become big problems.

Whether you're calculating revenue, estimating market size, or evaluating cost savings, you'll be using addition, subtraction, multiplication, and division frequently.

Arithmetic is the foundation of all other math in case interviews. If you're slow or inaccurate with basic arithmetic, everything else becomes harder.

On the other hand, if you're fast and confident with your arithmetic, you'll free up mental energy to focus on the more difficult parts of case math.

The goal of this chapter is to refresh your arithmetic skills and shake off any rust you may have from relying on spreadsheets and calculators.

Addition

You'll need to do addition in almost every case interview, whether it's adding revenues from multiple product lines or summing expenses.

Addition involves combining two or more numbers to find their total or sum.

Example #1: A company sells three products. Product A makes $400,000, Product B makes $350,000, and Product C makes $550,000. What's the company's total annual revenue?

Revenue = $400,000 + $350,000 + $550,000

Revenue = $1,300,000

The company's total annual revenue is $1,300,000.

Example #2: A company is launching a new snack product. Estimate the total monthly cost based on the following components:

- Raw materials: $120,000
- Packaging: $30,000
- Labor: $80,000
- Marketing: $50,000
- Distribution: $20,000

Costs = $120,000 + $30,000 + $80,000 + $50,000 + $20,000

Costs = $300,000

Total monthly costs are $300,000.

Subtraction

Subtraction frequently shows up in case interviews. For example, it's used when calculating profit, estimating savings, or calculating differences between scenarios.

Subtraction involves taking one number away from another to find the difference between them.

Example #1: A product sells for $20 and costs $8 to make. What is the profit per unit?

Profit = $20 - $8

Profit = $12

The profit per unit is $12.

Example #2: A company earns $1.2 million in revenue. It spends $250,000 on labor, $400,000 on materials, and $150,000 on overhead. What is their profit?

Profit = $1,200,000 - $250,000 - $400,000 - $150,000

Profit = $400,000

The company's profit is $400,000.

Multiplication

Multiplication is essential for calculating total revenues, converting units, and scaling things up. It is the repeated addition of the same number.

Example #1: Estimate how many cups of coffee are sold daily in a city if there are 1,000 coffee shops and each shop sells 150 cups per day.

Cups = 1,000 * 150

Cups = 150,000

150,000 cups are sold per day.

Example #2: A factory runs 16 hours per day, 6 days per week, and produces 450 units per hour. How many units does it produce in 4 weeks?

Output = 16 * 6 * 450 * 4

Output = 172,800 units

The factory produces 172,800 units in 4 weeks.

Division

Division is most commonly used to break down totals into per-unit or per-person figures. It is also used to calculate market shares and determine certain efficiency metrics.

Division involves splitting a number into equal parts or finding out how many times one number fits into another.

Example #1: A company spends $600,000 to produce 120,000 units. What is the cost per unit?

Cost per unit = $600,000 / 120,000

Cost per unit = $5

The cost per unit is $5.

Example #2: A logistics company spent $1.8M to transport 900,000 pounds of goods a total distance of 1,000 miles. What was the cost per pound per mile?

Cost per pound per mile = $1.8M / 900,000 pounds / 1,000 miles

Cost per pound per mile = $0.002

The cost per pound per mile is $0.002.

Summary

- Addition involves combining two or more numbers to find their total or sum

- Subtraction involves taking one number away from another to find the difference between them

- Multiplication is the repeated addition of the same number

- Division involves splitting a number into equal parts or finding out how many times one number fits into another

Practice Problems

1. 245 + 678
2. 3,216 + 1,789
3. 5,432 + 2,198 + 867
4. 1,000 − 475
5. 5,260 − 2,483
6. 10,000 − 3,432 − 1,568
7. 23 × 5
8. 128 × 6
9. 34 × 17
10. 56 × 43
11. 144 ÷ 12
12. 1,024 ÷ 16
13. 2,352 ÷ 28
14. 980 ÷ 7
15. (135 + 415) × 2
16. (1,000 − 250) ÷ 25
17. 3 × (456 − 231)
18. (720 ÷ 6) + 95
19. 300 + [(480 ÷ 8) × 3]

20. $(1{,}200 - 600) \div (20 - 10)$

Solutions

1. **923**
2. **5,005**
3. **8,497**
4. **525**
5. **2,777**
6. **5,000**
7. **115**
8. **768**
9. **578**
10. **2,408**
11. **12**
12. **64**
13. **84**
14. **140**
15. **1,100**
16. **30**
17. **675**
18. **215**
19. **480**

20. **60**

3. Fractions

What is a Fraction?

A fraction is a way of expressing a part of a whole. It consists of two numbers:

- Numerator (top number): How many parts you have

- Denominator (bottom number): How many parts the whole is divided into

An example of a fraction is 3/4, which means 3 parts out of 4 equal parts.

In case interviews, fractions appear in many ways:

- Calculating profit margins (e.g., profit / revenue)

- Estimating market share (e.g., company revenue / total market revenue)

- Working with ratios and proportions (we'll cover these later)

It you can confidently work with fractions, you'll find it easier to handle a wide range of case interview math problems.

Simplifying Fractions

Simplifying a fraction means reducing it to the smallest equivalent form. For example, the simplified form of 8/16 is 1/2.

1/2 is equal to 8/16 and is the simplified form because the numerator and denominator are expressed in the smallest numbers possible.

You typically want to simplify fractions because smaller numbers in fractions are easier to work with.

There are three steps to simplifying a fraction:

1. List all of the factors of the numerator and denominator. A factor is a number that divides another number exactly, with no remainder.

2. Find the greatest common factor of the numerator and denominator

3. Divide both the numerator and denominator by that number

Example #1: Simplify 8/12.

First, let's find all the factors of the numerator and denominator.

The factors of 8 are: 1, 2, 4, 8.

The factors of 12 are: 1, 2, 3, 4, 6, 12.

Based on this, the greatest common factor is 4 because it is the largest factor that shows up in both the numerator and denominator.

Now, we can divide the numerator and denominator by the greatest common factor.

Numerator: 8 ÷ 4 = 2.

Denominator: 12 ÷ 4 = 3.

Therefore, 8/12 simplifies to 2/3.

Example #2: Simplify 45/60.

The factors of 45 are: 1, 3, 5, 9, 15, 45.

The factors of 60 are: 1, 2, 3, 4, 5, 6, 10, 12, 15, 20, 30, 60.

The greatest common factor is 15.

Numerator: 45 ÷ 15 = 3.

Denominator: 60 ÷ 15 = 4.

Therefore, 45/60 simplifies to 3/4.

Another way to simplify fractions is to divide the numerator and denominator by any number that both the numerator and denominator are divisible by.

You can repeat this until there are no more numbers that the numerator and denominator can be divided by evenly.

Example #3: Simplify 72/136.

Let's divide the numerator and denominator by 2 to get 36/68.

We can divide the numerator and denominator again by 2 to get 18/34.

We can divide the numerator and denominator for a third time by 2 to get 9/17.

There are no more numbers that both the numerator and denominator can be divided by evenly, so 9/17 is our final answer.

Adding Fractions

Fractions can only be added if the denominators are the same. If that is the case, simply add the numerators and keep the same denominator to get your answer.

Example #1: 3/8 + 1/8

Since the denominators of both fractions are the same, all we need to do is add the numerators. So, we get 4/8, which simplifies to 1/2.

However, if the denominators of two fractions are different, there are a few more steps needed:

1. Find a common denominator

2. Adjust each fraction to have that denominator

3. Add the numerators

4. Simplify the fraction if needed

To find a common denominator, list out the multiples of each denominator. Multiples are the result of multiplying a number by whole numbers (e.g., 1, 2, 3, 4).

Then, find the smallest multiple that all the denominators share. That will be your common denominator.

Example #2: 1/4 + 1/3

The multiples of 4 are: 4, 8, 12, 16, 20…

The multiples of 3 are: 3, 6, 9, 12, 15…

The smallest multiple that appears in both lists is 12. So, that will be our common denominator.

1/4 can be rewritten as 3/12.

1/3 can be rewritten as 4/12.

Now, we can add 3/12 + 4/12.

This gives us our answer, 7/12.

If you don't want to find the smallest common multiple, you can always find a common denominator by multiplying all of the denominators.

Example #3: 1/4 + 2/3 + 1/5

Multiplying all of the denominators gets us 4 * 3 * 5 = 60. This is a common denominator we can use.

The fractions can be re-written as: 15/60 + 40/60 + 12/60.

This gives us our answer: 67/60.

Subtracting Fractions

Subtracting fractions works exactly the same as adding fractions.

1. Find a common denominator
2. Adjust each fraction to have that denominator
3. Subtract the numerators
4. Simplify the fraction if needed

Example #1: 3/4 – 1/2

The multiples of 4 are: 4, 8, 12…

The multiples of 2 are: 2, 4, 8…

The smallest common denominator is 4.

Rewriting the fractions: 3/4 – 2/4 = 1/4.

Example #2: 5/6 – 1/4

If we don't want to find the smallest common multiple, we can just multiply the denominators to get a common denominator.

6 * 4 = 24

Re-writing the fractions: 20/24 – 6/24 = 14/24.

This simplifies to 7/12.

Multiplying Fractions

Multiplying fractions is much easier than adding or subtracting fractions. You won't need to find a common denominator.

There are three steps to multiplying fractions:

1. Multiply the numerators
2. Multiply the denominators
3. Simplify the fraction if needed

Example #1: 2/3 * 3/4

Multiplying the numerators: 2 * 3 = 6

Multiplying the denominators 3 * 4 = 12

This gives us 6/12, which can be simplified to 1/2.

Let's take a look at another example.

Example #2: 5/8 * 4/10

Multiplying the numerators: 5 * 4 = 20

Multiplying the denominators: 8 * 10 = 80

This gives us 20/80, which can be simplified to 1/4.

Dividing Fractions

Dividing fractions is just as easy as multiplying fractions, but it involves one extra step.

1. Flip the second fraction. This is known as taking its reciprocal.
2. Multiply the numerators
3. Multiply the denominators
4. Simplify the fraction if needed

Example #1: 3/4 ÷ 1/2

The first step is to rewrite this as: 3/4 * 2/1

Multiplying the numerators: 3 * 2 = 6

Multiplying the denominators: 4 * 1 = 4

6/4 simplifies to 3/2

Let's take a look at another example.

Example #2: 5/6 ÷ 10/9

5/6 * 9/10

45/60

3/4

Summary

- A fraction is a way of expressing a part of a whole. It consists of two numbers:
    - Numerator (top number): How many parts you have
    - Denominator (bottom number): How many parts the whole is divided into
- Simplifying a fraction means reducing it to the smallest equivalent form, where the numerator and denominator are expressed in the smallest numbers possible
- To add or subtract fractions, adjust each fraction to have the same denominator and then add or subtract the numerators while keeping the denominator
- To multiply fractions, multiply the numerators and denominators
- To divide fractions, flip the second fraction and multiply the numerators and denominators

Practice Problems

1. Simplify 18/24
2. Simplify 45/60
3. 1/4 + 1/2
4. 5/6 + 2/3
5. 7/10 + 9/15
6. 5/6 – 1/3
7. 11/12 – 5/8
8. 9/10 – 2/5
9. 3/4 * 2/5
10. 7/9 * 6/14
11. 8/15 * 10/12
12. 3/5 ÷ 2/3
13. 7/8 ÷ 14/15
14. 9/10 ÷ 3/4
15. (3/7 ÷ 2/5) * (4/3 + 1/6)

Solutions

1. **3/4**
2. **3/4**
3. **3/4**
4. **3/2**
5. **13/10**
6. **1/2**
7. **7/24**
8. **1/2**
9. **3/10**
10. **1/3**
11. **4/9**
12. **9/10**
13. **15/16**
14. **6/5**
15. **45/28**

4. Decimals

What is a Decimal?

A decimal is another way to express parts of a whole, just like fractions. They key difference is that decimals use powers of 10 and are written with a decimal point.

For example:

- 0.5 means 5 parts out of 10 equal parts

- 0.25 means 25 parts out of 100 equal parts

- 0.125 means 125 parts out of 1000 equal parts

The number to the left of the decimal point is the whole number part while the number to the right of the decimal point is the fractional part.

For example, the number 123.456 can be thought of as 123 + 456/1,000.

Being comfortable with decimals will help you move faster and more confidently in your case interviews.

Adding Decimals

There are three steps to adding decimals:

1. Line up the decimal points

2. Add from right to left, just like whole numbers

3. Keep the decimal point in the same position in your answer

Example #1: 2.3 + 1.4

These two decimal points are already lined up because both decimals only go to the tenths. Therefore, we can just add these numbers up as if they were whole numbers and keep the decimal point in the same place.

2.3 + 1.4 = 3.7

Example #2: 0.75 + 1.2

These two decimal points are not lined up. 0.75 goes to the hundredths while 1.2 only goes to the tenths.

So, we need to line up the decimal points by rewriting this as:

0.75 + 1.20 = 1.95

Subtracting Decimals

Subtracting decimals follows the exact same steps as adding. However, as with normal subtraction with whole numbers, you may need to borrow from the column on the left.

Here's how to subtract decimals:

1. Line up the decimal points
2. Subtract from right to left
3. Borrow if necessary
4. Keep the decimal point in the same spot

Example #1: 3.6 – 1.2

The decimal points are already lined up, so we just need to subtract.

3.6 – 1.2 = 2.4

Example #2: 2.05 – 0.8

The decimal points are not lined up, so we need to rewrite this as:

2.05 – 0.80 = 1.25

Multiplying Decimals

Multiplying decimals involves just three steps:

1. Ignore decimals at first and just multiply like whole numbers
2. Count the total number of decimal places in both numbers
3. Place the decimal in the product with that many places

Example #1: 0.3 * 0.2

Ignoring the decimals, 3 * 2 = 6.

There is 1 decimal place in each number, for a total of 2 decimal places.

So, we take the product of 6 and move the decimal point over two places.

The final answer is 0.06.

Let's take a look at another example.

Example #2: 2.5 * 0.35

25 * 35 = 875

There are a total of 3 decimal places across the two numbers. So, we need to move the decimal point over 3 places.

Our final answer is 0.875.

Dividing Decimals

Dividing decimals requires a little bit more work than multiplying. Follow these steps to divide decimals:

1. Move the decimal in the divisor (the number you're dividing by) to make it a whole number

2. Move the decimal in the dividend (the number being divided) the same number of places

3. Divide as normal

Example #1: 0.6 ÷ 0.25

0.25 is the divisor. To make it a whole number, we need to move the decimal point over 2 places.

0.6 is the dividend. We'll need to move the decimal point over the same number of places as we did for the divisor.

So, this calculation can be rewritten as:

60 ÷ 25 = 2.4

Let's take a look at another example.

Example #2:

0.125 ÷ 0.08

0.08 needs to be rewritten as 8, which involves moving the decimal point over 2 places.

Moving the decimal point in 0.125 over 2 places gets us 12.5.

So, this calculation can be rewritten as:

12.5 ÷ 8 = 1.5625

Converting Between Decimals and Fractions

During your case interview, it may be helpful to convert decimals to fractions. In certain situations, this could make calculations easier.

To do this, there are three steps:

1. Identify the place value of the last digit
2. Place the decimal over its place value
3. Simplify the fraction if necessary

Example #1: Convert 0.75 to a fraction

75/100 = 3/4

Example #2: Convery 0.125 as a fraction

125/1000 = 1/8

Summary

- A decimal is another way to express parts of a whole using powers of 10 and a decimal point

- To add or subtract decimals, line up the decimal points

- To multiply decimals, multiply like whole numbers and then place the decimal based on the total number of decimal places in both numbers

- To divide decimals, move the decimal in the divisor (the number you're dividing by) to make it a whole number and move the decimal in the dividend (the number being divided) the same number of places

- To convert between decimals and fractions, identify the place value of the last digit and place the decimal over its place value

Practice Problems

1. 12.75 + 8.9

2. 3.456 + 7.08 + 1.004

3. 15.6 − 9.85

4. 100.25 − 47.938

5. 4.2 × 3.5

6. 1.75 × 0.6

7. 23.08 × 0.1

8. 45.5 ÷ 5

9. 7.2 ÷ 0.3

10. 8.4 ÷ 1.2

11. (4.5 + 2.3) × 0.4

12. (12.8 − 4.3) ÷ 2.5

13. (3.75 × 2) − 1.5

14. Convert 0.55 to a simplified fraction

15. Convert 0.375 to a simplified fraction

Solutions

1. **21.65**
2. **11.54**
3. **5.75**
4. **52.312**
5. **14.7**
6. **1.05**
7. **2.308**
8. **9.1**
9. **24**
10. 7
11. **2.72**
12. **3.4**
13. 6
14. **11/20**
15. **3/8**

5. Percentages

What is a Percentage?

A percentage is a way of expressing a number as a part of 100. The word "percent" literally means "per hundred."

In addition to fractions and decimals, percentages are a way to express parts of a whole.

For example:

- 25% means 25 out of 100
- 50% means 50 out of 100
- 100% means 100 out of 100

In case interviews, percentages are everywhere. You'll use them to:

- Calculate profit margins
- Estimate growth rates

- Compare year-over-year performance

If you're fast and confident with percentages, you'll handle case interview math more efficiently.

Converting Between Percentages and Decimals

To convert a percentage to a decimal, simply divide by 100. A shortcut to doing this is by moving the decimal point two places to the left.

Example #1: Express 25% as a decimal

25/100 = 0.25

Let's take a look at another example.

Example #2: Express 150% as a decimal.

150/100 = 1.5

To convert a decimal to a percentage, multiply by 100. A shortcut to doing this is by moving the decimal two places to the right.

Example #1: Express 0.3 as a percentage

0.3 * 100% = 30%

Let's take a look at another example.

Example #2: Express 1.25 as a percentage

1.25 * 100% = 125%

Converting Between Percentages and Fractions

Many common percentages have simple fractional equivalents. Knowing these helps speed up your math during a case interview.

Here are some conversions you should be familiar with:

- 10% = 1/10
- 12.5% = 1/8
- 20% = 1/5
- 25% = 1/4
- 33.333% = 1/3
- 37.5% = 3/8
- 40% = 2/5
- 50% = 1/2
- 60% = 3/5
- 62.5% = 5/8
- 66.666% = 2/3
- 75% = 3/4
- 80% = 4/5
- 87.5% = 7/8
- 100% = 1

Percent Change Formula

Percent change is an important formula for case interviews. It measures how much something has increased or decreased relative to its original value.

Here is the formula:

Percent Change = (New Value – Old Value) / Old Value * 100%

There are so many different applications of the percent change formula in case interviews. For example, it is used to calculate things such as growth, discounts, and interest.

Example #1: Revenue grew from $100M to $120M. What is the percent change?

Percent Change = (New Value – Old Value) / Old Value * 100%

Percent Change = ($120M - $100M) / $100M * 100%

Percent Change = $20M / $100M * 100%

Percent Change = 20%

Example #2: The price of a product is lowered from $200 to $150. What is the percent discount?

Percent Change = (New Value – Old Value) / Old Value * 100%

Percent Change = ($150 – $200) / $200 * 100%

Percent Change = -$50 / $200 * 100%

Percent Change = -25%

Percentage Change vs. Percentage Point

There is an important distinction that you need to know between two terms that sound similar, but are completely different.

Percentage change is a relative change. It measures the change relative to the original starting value.

Percentage point measures an absolute change. It measures the difference between the new value and the original value.

Example #1: A company's revenue growth rate is expected to increase from 5% to 7%. How much of an increase is this?

Percent Change = (New Value - Old Value) / Old Value * 100%

Percent Change = (7% - 5%) / 5% * 100%

Percent Change = 2% / 5% * 100%

Percent Change = 40%

This is a 40% increase in relative terms.

Percentage Point Change = 7% - 5%

Percentage Point Change = 2%

You could also say that this is a 2 percentage point increase in absolute terms.

Example #2: A company's profit margin has declined from 16% to 12%. How much of a decrease is this?

Percent Change = (New Value - Old Value) / Old Value * 100%

Percent Change = (12% - 16%) / 16% * 100%

Percent Change = -4% / 16% * 100%

Percent Change = -25%

This is a 25% decrease in relative terms.

Percentage Point Change = 12% - 16%

Percentage Point Change = -4%

You could also say that this is a 4 percentage point decrease in absolute terms.

Compound Annual Growth Rate

There is another important concept you should be familiar with called the compound annual growth rate, or CAGR for short.

CAGR tells you the average yearly growth rate over a period of time, assuming the growth was steady every year.

It's a way to smooth out ups and downs and see how fast something grew overall. It is used to compare growth between different business units, markets, or time periods.

You most likely won't need to calculate a CAGR in a case interview. However, you'll need to be familiar with how to interpret one.

Here's the formula to calculate a CAGR:

CAGR = (Ending Value / Beginning Value)$^{1/\text{Number of Years}}$ − 1

Example #1: A company's revenue grew from $10M to $80M in 3 years. On average, how much did the company grow per year over this time period?

CAGR = (Ending Value / Beginning Value)$^{1/\text{Number of Years}}$ − 1

CAGR = ($80M / $10M)$^{1/3}$ − 1

CAGR = 100%

The company grew by 100% each year over this time period.

Example #2: A streaming platform currently has 100,000 paid subscribers. After 4 years, they have 8.1 million paid subscribers. What is the CAGR over this time period?

CAGR = (Ending Value / Beginning Value)$^{1/\text{Number of Years}}$ − 1

CAGR = ($8.1M / $100K)$^{1/4}$ − 1

CAGR = 200%

The streaming platform's CAGR is 200% over this time period.

Summary

- A percentage is a way of expressing a number as a part of 100

- To convert a percentage to a decimal, divide by 100 or move the decimal point two places to the left

- Many common percentages have simple fractional equivalents that are helpful to know to speed up your math

- Percent Change = (New Value − Old Value) / Old Value * 100%

- Percentage change is a relative change, measuring the change relative to the original starting value

- Percentage point measures an absolute change, measuring the difference between the new value and the original value

- CAGR tells you the average yearly growth rate over a period of time, assuming the growth was steady every year

- CAGR = (Ending Value / Beginning Value)$^{1/\text{Number of Years}}$ − 1

Practice Problems

1. Convert 42% to a decimal

2. Convert 0.06 to a percentage

3. Convert 125% to a decimal

4. Convert 75% to a simplified fraction

5. Convert 3/5 to a percentage

6. Convert 12.5% to a fraction in simplest form

7. A product's price increased from $40 to $50. What is the percent change?

8. A company's revenue dropped from $500K to $425K. What is the percent change?

9. A subscription increased from $16 to $20. What is the percent change?

10. A politician's approval rating went from 30% to 40%. What is the percentage point change? What is the percent change?

11. A bank raised its interest rate from 2% to 3%. What is the percentage point change? What is the percent change?

12. A user base grew from 1,000 to 8,000 in 3 years. What is the CAGR?

Solutions

1. **0.42**
2. **6%**
3. **1.25**
4. **3/4**
5. **60%**
6. **1/8**
7. **25%**
8. **-15%**
9. **25%**
10. **10 percentage point increase and 33.333% (rounded) increase**
11. **1 percentage point increase and 50% increase**
12. **100%**

6. Ratios and Proportions

What is a Ratio?

A ratio is a way to compare two or more quantities. It tells you how much of one thing there is compared to another.

Ratios can be written in three ways:

- As "A to B"
- With a colon
- As a fraction

For example, if a company has 5 designers and 10 engineers, the ratio of designers to engineers is:

- 5 to 10
- 5:10
- 5/10

Just like fractions, ratios can be simplified. In the previous example, the ratio can be simplified to:

- 1 to 2
- 1:2
- 1/2

There are two different types of ratios you should be familiar with.

The first type are part-to-part ratios, which compare two distinct groups that are both part of a whole.

For example, in a company with 2 male employees and 3 female employees, the ratio of males to females is 2:3.

The second type of ratio are part-to-whole ratios, which compare one group to the total.

For example, in a company with 2 male employees and 3 female employees, the total number of employees is 5. The ratio of males to total employees is 2:5.

Ratios show up frequently in case interviews, particularly in market share analyses, cost breakdowns, and scaling calculations. Look for these clues to know when to use ratios:

- You're asked to scale things up or down
- You're given part-to-part or part-to-whole information
- You're comparing different segments or groups
- You need to allocate totals

Example #1: A company has three products that generate a total of $500M in revenue.

- Product A generates $125M in revenue

- Product B generates $175M in revenue
- Product C generates $200M in revenue

What is the ratio of revenue across Product A, Product B, and Product C?

We can take the products' revenue figures and express them as a ratio.

125:175:200

This ratio can be simplified by dividing each number by 25.

The ratio of revenue is 5:7:8.

Let's take a look at another example.

Example #2: A company's total production cost is $120 per unit.

- 60% is raw materials
- 25% is labor
- 15% is overhead

What is the cost ratio between raw materials and labor?

We can get the cost ratio by taking a ratio of the percentage of costs that raw materials and labor make up of the total per unit cost.

60:25

This can be simplified by dividing both numbers by 5.

The cost ratio is 12:5.

What is a Proportion?

A proportion is an equation that states two ratios are equal.

For example, 1/2 = 2/4 is an example of a proportion.

In case math, proportions are used for solving unknown values, especially when you're told that something scales or grows evenly.

To solve a proportion, there are three steps:

1. Set up the ratio you're given

2. Set up a second ratio with the unknown

3. Cross-multiply and solve for the unknown

Here's a refresher on cross-multiplying.

If you have: a/b = c/d, then cross-multiplying gives: a * d = b * c.

You are essentially multiplying both sides of the equation by the denominators to eliminate the fractions. Cross-multiplying is a shortcut to do this in a single step.

Example #1: 3 out of 5 customers buy online. If you expect to have 20 customers, how many would you expect to buy online?

3 / 5 = x / 20

3 * 20 = 5 * x

x = 12

We'd expect 12 customers to buy online.

Let's take a look at another example.

Example #2: If a factory produces 40 units in 8 hours, how many units can the factory produce in 12 hours?

$40 / 8 = x / 12$

$40 * 12 = 8 * x$

$x = 60$

The factory can produce 60 units in 12 hours.

Summary

- A ratio is a way to compare two or more quantities by showing how much of one thing there is compared to another

- Ratios can be written in three ways:
    - As "A to B"
    - With a colon
    - As a fraction

- A proportion is an equation that states two ratios are equal

- Cross-multiply to solve proportions: if a/b = c/d, then a * d = b * c

Practice Problems

1. A company has 2 salespeople in Region A and 3 in Region B. If Region A brings in $400K in sales and Region B brings in $900K, what is the sales per salesperson ratio between Region A and Region B?

2. A factory produces 1,200 units with 20 workers. At the same rate, how many units would 30 workers produce?

3. A marketing budget of $120,000 is split between three regions in a 2:3:5 ratio. How much does each region receive?

4. A team of analysts finishes 60 reports in 15 hours. At the same rate, how long would it take to finish 100 reports?

5. A product sells for $24 and the cost to produce it is $18. What is the cost-to-price ratio?

6. If a project manager is paid in the ratio of 3:2 compared to an analyst, and the analyst is paid $60K per year, how much is the project manager paid?

7. A consulting firm has 12 juniors and 8 seniors. What is the ratio of juniors to the total team?

8. Three teams are staffed in the ratio 4:5:6. If there are 90 people in total, how many people are on each team?

Solutions

1. **2 to 3**

    Region A: $400K / 2 = $200K per salesperson

    Region B: $900K / 3 = $300K per salesperson

    $200K to $300K = 2 to 3

2. **1,800 units**

    1,200 units / 20 workers = 60 units per worker

    60 units per worker * 30 workers = 1,800 units

3. **$24K, $36K, and $60K**

    Ratio total = 2 + 3 + 5 = 10 parts

    $120K / 10 parts = $12K per part

    Region 1 = 2 * $12K = $24K

    Region 2 = 3 * $12K = $36K

    Region 3 = 5 * $12K = $60K

4. **25 hours**

    60 reports / 15 hours = 4 reports per hour

    100 reports / 4 reports per hour = 25 hours

5. **3 to 4**

    $18 to $24 simplifies to 3 to 4

6. **$90K**

2 parts = $60K

1 part = $30K

3 parts * $30K = $90K

7. **3 to 5**

    12 to (12 + 8)

    12 to 20

    Simplifies to 3 to 5

8. **24, 30 and 36**

    4 + 5 + 6 = 15 parts

    90 people / 15 parts = 6 people per part

    Team A = 4 * 6 = 24

    Team B = 5 * 6 = 30

    Team C = 6 * 6 = 36

7. Statistics

Why Statistics Matter

Statistics is the math behind collecting, analyzing, and interpreting data. It helps make sense of data.

Consulting is all about making sense of messy data. In a case interview, you'll have to do the same when solving quantitative problems.

The good news is that you don't need to memorize any complicated formulas. There are only a few basic concepts in statistics that you need to know:

- Average
- Weighted average
- Standard deviation
- Minimum, maximum, and range
- Percentiles

- Probability

- Expected value

We'll cover each of these topics in this chapter.

Average

The average, or mean, is a number that represents the middle or typical value in a group of numbers.

The formula to calculate the average is:

Average = Sum of all values / Number of values

Example #1: A company's five regional offices generated sales of $10M, $12M, $15M, $13M, and $20M. What are the average sales per office?

Average = Sum of all values / Number of values

Average = ($10M + $12M + $15M + $13M + $20M) / 5

Average = $14M

Example #2: The daily utilization of a factory this week was 80%, 85%, 90%, 95%, and 100%. What is its average utilization?

Average = Sum of all values / Number of values

Average = (80% + 85% + 90% + 95% + 100%) / 5

Average = 90%

Weighted Average

Not all data points contribute equally to the average. When some values contribute more than others, a weighted average is used.

The formula to calculate a weighted average is:

Weighted average = $(v_1 * w_1) + (v_2 * w_2) + ... / (w_1 + w_2 + ...)$

In this formula, v represents the different values and w represents the different weights.

Explained in simpler terms, the weighted average is calculated by multiplying each value by its weight, summing up all of these products, and then dividing by the total weight.

Although the weighted average formula looks complicated, it should feel simple and intuitive to you.

Example #1: Suppose a retailer has two stores:

- Store A: 100 customers spending $10 each
- Store B: 50 customers spending $30 each

To find the average spend per customer, you can't just take the average of $10 and $30 because there are a different number of customers that spent these amounts.

You need to weight these values by the number of customers.

In this example, the values are the spending amounts and the weights are the number of customers.

Weighted average = [(100 * $10) + (50 * $30)] / (100 + 50)

Weighted average = $16.67 (rounded)

The average spend per customer is $16.67.

Example #2: A company operates in three regions. Each region conducts customer surveys and reports an average satisfaction score out of 10. However, each region has a different number of customers surveyed.

- North region: 100 customers surveyed, 8.5 average score
- South region: 300 customers surveyed, 8.0 average score
- West region: 100 customers surveyed, 9.0 average score

What is the overall average customer satisfaction score?

We can't just take the average of the three average scores because there are a different number of customers surveyed in each region.

We need to use the weighted average formula.

In this example, the values are the average scores and the weights are the number of customers surveyed.

Weighted average = [(100 * 8.5) + (300 * 8.0) + (100 * 9.0)] / (100 + 300 + 100)

Weighted average = 8.3

The overall average customer satisfaction score is 8.3.

Median

The median is the middle value in a dataset when arranged in order from smallest to largest.

Finding the median is simple:

1. Put the numbers in order from smallest to largest
2. If there's an odd number of values, the median is the middle number

3. If there's an even number of values, the median is the average of the two most middle numbers

Similar to an average, the median measures the middle or typical value in a group of numbers. However, unlike an average, the median is not affected by extreme outliers.

If there's a single number that is extremely small or large compared to the other numbers, this will greatly affect what the average is. However, this will have much less of an impact on the median.

So, if there is a data set that has extreme outliers, the median may be a better measure of the middle or typical value.

Example #1: A company has three sales representatives that have made 7, 1, and 4 sales this week. What is the median number of sales made per representative? What is the average number of sales made per representative?

Arranging the number of sales in order from smallest to largest gives: 1, 4, and 7.

The middle number is 4, which is the median.

Average = (7 + 1 + 4) / 3

Average = 4

Coincidentally, the average number of sales is also 4.

Let's take a look at another example.

Example #2: A company has three sales representatives that have made 100, 1, and 4 sales this week. What is the median number of sales made per representative? What is the average number of sales made per representative?

Arranging the number of sales in order from smallest to largest gives: 1, 4, and 100.

The middle number is 4, which is the median. Notice that the median has not changed from the previous example.

Average = (100 + 1 + 4) / 3

Average = 35

The average number of sales is 35.

This example illustrates the differences between the average and the median. The median is not affected as much by extreme outliers while the average is greatly affected.

Standard Deviation

Standard deviation measures how spread out numbers are from the average.

A low standard deviation means values are tightly clustered around the average while a high standard deviation means values are more spread out.

In a case interview, you won't ever need to calculate the standard deviation, but understanding what it is conceptually will be helpful.

In a case interview, standard deviation can be used to:

- Assess risk or variability

- Understand customer behavior

- Measure operational performance

- Benchmark performance

- Forecast or estimate future outcomes

Example #1: Two products each generate $100K per month in revenue. However, Product A has a standard deviation of $5K per month while Product B has a standard deviation of $30K per month. What can you conclude from this?

Product A has more consistent monthly sales. Product B is more unpredictable. The company should prioritize selling Product A if they prefer revenue stability.

Let's take a look at another example.

Example #2: A client runs 10 marketing campaigns. The average profit per campaign is $50K with a standard deviation of $100K. What can you conclude from this?

Some campaigns perform very well, while others perform poorly. Results are very inconsistent. The client should consider reallocating budget to the best-performing campaigns.

Minimum, Maximum, and Range

The minimum, or min, is the smallest value in a dataset. The maximum, or max, is the largest value in a dataset.

The range is the difference between the maximum and minimum.

These metrics are used to understand variability and compare consistency between two things.

Example: Daily sales this week were: $1K, $2K, $2.5K, $3K, and $5K. What is the minimum, maximum, and range?

The minimum is the smallest value, $1K.

The maximum is the largest value, $5K.

The range is the difference between these two, $5K - $1K = $4K.

Percentiles

Percentiles tell you how a value compares to the rest of the values. It is defined as the percentage of values that fall below a certain number.

For example, if something is in the 90th percentile, that means that 90% of all other values fall below it.

Percentiles are primarily used in case interviews when benchmarking performance to see how something compares to others. It can also be used to understand distributions in graphs.

Example #1: Store A's sales is in the top 25%. What percentile is it?

Store A is in the 75th percentile since 75% of stores perform worse than it.

Let's take a look at another example.

Example #2: Store B's sales is the median sales out of 100 stores. What percentile is it?

Store B is in the 50th percentile because the median is the middle value. Half of the other stores have higher sales while the other half have lower sales.

There are a few special types of percentiles you should be familiar with.

Quartiles divide the data into four parts, each making up 25%.

- First quartile = 0th to 25th percentile
- Second quartile = 25th to 50th percentile
- Third quartile = 50th to 75th percentile
- Fourth quartile = 75th to 100th percentile

Deciles divide the data into ten parts, each making up 10%.

- First decile = 0th to 10th percentile
- Second decile = 10th to 20th percentile
- Third decile = 20th to 30th percentile
- Fourth decile = 30th to 40th percentile
- Fifth decile = 40th to 50th percentile
- Sixth decile = 50th to 60th percentile
- Seventh decile = 60th to 70th percentile
- Eighth decile = 70th to 80th percentile
- Ninth decile = 80th to 90th percentile
- Tenth decile = 90th to 100th percentile

Probability

Probability is the likelihood that something will happen, expressed as a value between 0% and 100%. It shows up in case interviews in a few different ways:

- Estimating the likelihood of success
- Choosing between uncertain options
- Predicting future scenarios

The only formula you need to know for probability is:

Probability = Favorable outcomes / Total possible outcomes

Example #1: If 30 out of 150 product launches have succeeded, what is the probability of a product launch succeeding?

Probability = Favorable outcomes / Total possible outcomes

Probability = 30 / 150

Probability = 0.2

There is a 20% chance of a product launch succeeding.

Let's take a look at another example.

Example #2: A company receives shipments of cookies from two suppliers.

- Supplier A provides 80% of all cookies and 5% of them are typically defective

- Supplier B provides 20% of all cookies and 10% of them are typically defective

An employee randomly inspects one cookie and it turns out to be defective. What is the probability that this defective cookie came from Supplier B?

To determine this, let's say that we have 100 cookies.

Supplier A provides 80 of these cookies. 5% of these cookies are defective, so 80 * 5% = 4 cookies are defective.

Supplier B provides 20 of these cookies. 10% of these are defective, so 20 * 10% = 2 cookies are defective.

Probability = 2 / (4 + 2)

Probability = 1/3

There is a 1/3 chance that the defective cookie came from Supplier B.

Expected Value

Expected value combines probability and outcomes to tell you the average result over time.

In other words, if a simulation was run a large number of times, the expected value would be the average result of all of the different results from the simulation.

The formula for expected value is:

Expected Value = $(P_1 * V_1) + (P_2 * V_2) + (P_3 * V_3) + ...$

In this formula, P = probability and V = value.

The formula may look complicated but all it is doing is taking the probability of each event and multiplying with the value or outcome of each event.

These products are all added together to get the expected value.

Example #1: A company launches a product that has a 30% chance to earn $5M and a 70% chance to lose $1M. What is the expected value of launching this product?

Expected Value = (0.3 * $5M) + (0.7 * -$1M)

Expected Value = $0.8M

The product launch has an expected value of $800K.

Let's take a look at another example.

Example #2: A company is considering launching a referral program. It expects that 50% of customers that participate in the program will generate 1 referral, 30% of customers will generate 2 referrals, and 20% of customers will generate 3 referrals. What is the average number of referrals that each customer will generate?

Expected Value = (50% * 1) + (30% * 2) + (20% * 3)

Expected Value = 1.7

Each customer will generate 1.7 referrals on average.

Summary

- Average = Sum of all values / Number of values

- Weighted average = $(v_1 \ast w_1) + (v_2 \ast w_2) + \ldots / (w_1 + w_2 + \ldots)$, where v represents the different values and w represents the different weights

- The median is the middle value in a dataset when arranged in order from smallest to largest

- Standard deviation measures how spread out numbers are from the average

- The minimum is the smallest value in a dataset, the maximum is the largest value in a dataset, and the range is the difference between the maximum and minimum

- Percentiles tell you how a value compares to the rest of the values, telling you the percentage of values that fall below a certain number

- Probability = Favorable outcomes / Total possible outcomes

- Expected Value = $(P_1 \ast V_1) + (P_2 \ast V_2) + (P_3 \ast V_3) + \ldots$, where P represents the probabilities of different events and V represents the values of the different events

Practice Problems

1. A company sold 120, 150, and 180 units in the last three months. What was the average number of units sold per month?

2. A student scored 82, 90, 88, and 75 on four tests. How many points do they need on a 5th test to have an average of 85?

3. A company has two divisions. Division A contributes 70% of revenue with an average profit margin of 30%. Division B contributes 30% of revenue with an average profit margin of 20%. What is the company's overall profit margin?

4. A consultant splits time across 3 clients:

   Client 1: 40% of time, billed at $200/hour

   Client 2: 35% of time, billed at $250/hour

   Client 3: 25% of time, billed at $300/hour

   What is the consultant's weighted average hourly rate?

5. Two teams have the following scores in a game:

   Team A: 50, 52, 48, 51, 49

   Team B: 40, 60, 30, 70, 20

   Which team has a higher standard deviation?

6. A store recorded daily sales of: $250, $300, $275, $400, and $350. What is the max, min, and range of sales?

7. A retailer tracks order values. The 90th percentile order value is $500. If 2,000 orders were placed, how many orders were below $500?

8. A box has 4 red, 3 blue, and 3 green balls. If one ball is drawn at random, what is the probability of drawing a red or blue ball?

9. A venture capitalist is investing in a startup. There is a 50% chance of making $1M, 30% chance of making $500K, and 20% chance of losing $250K. What is the expected return on investment?

10. A lottery ticket has a 1% chance to win $100 and a 99% chance to win nothing. What's the expected value?

Solutions

1. **150 units per month**

    Average = (120 + 150 + 180) / 3 = 150

2. **90**

    To have an average of 85 over 5 tests, the total score needs to be 85 * 5 = 425

    Score on 5th test = 425 − (82 + 90 + 88 + 75) = 90

3. **27% profit margin**

    Overall profit margin = (70% * 30%) + (30% * 20%) = 27%

4. **$242.50 per hour**

    Average hourly rate = (40% * $200) + (35% * $250) + (25% * $300) = $242.50

5. **Team B has higher standard deviation**

    Team B has a wider range of scores while Team A's scores are much closer together

6. **Max: $400, Min: $250, Range: $150**

    The largest value is $400 and the smallest value is $250

    Range = Max − Min = $400 − $250 = $150

7. **1,800 orders**

    90% * 2,000 = 1,800

8. **70%**

    (4 + 3) / 10 = 7/10 = 70%

9. **$600K**

    Expected value = (50% * $1M) + (30% * $500K) + [20% * (-$250K)] = $600K

10. **$1**

    Expected value = (1% * $100) + (99% * $0) = $1

Taylor Warfield

8. Algebra

Why Algebra Matters

Algebra is a way of solving problems by using letters to stand for unknown numbers and then figuring out what those numbers are.

Algebra shows up in case interviews all the time. Whether you're calculating breakeven points, estimating profits, or figuring out how price affects demand, you're going to be solving for unknown numbers.

Having a solid understanding of basic algebra will give you the tools to solve case interview problems quickly and confidently. It'll help you:

- Understand relationships among different numbers
- Simplify complex problems into manageable equations
- Analyze different scenarios
- Facilitate logical reasoning

What is a Variable?

A variable is just a symbol, usually a letter such as x, that stands for a number that you don't know. Examples of commonly used variables include:

- p = price
- q = quantity
- t = time
- π = profit
- g = growth rate

In a case interview, it doesn't matter what letter you use to represent an unknown variable. So, pick one that makes the most sense to you for the given situation.

Translating Business Language into Algebra

In order to solve for an unknown number, you'll need to write an equation first.

A huge part of algebra in case interviews is taking a word problem and turning it into an equation. Here are a few examples of turning words into an equation.

Example #1: A company sells 1,000 units of a product and generates $50,000 in revenue. What is the price per unit?

Revenue = Quantity * Price

$50,000 = 1,000 * p

Let's take a look at another example.

Example #2: A company sells a product for $120 and makes a $50 profit on each sale. What is the cost to produce the product?

Profit = Price − Cost

$50 = $120 − c

Let's take a look at our last example.

Example #3: A company currently spends $200,000 per month on marketing and acquires 5,000 new users per month. They are considering launching a more targeted campaign that would cost $250,000 per month.

How many new users would this new campaign need to bring in to keep the same cost per acquired customer?

$200,000 / 5,000 = $250,000 / x

How to Solve for a Single Unknown Variable

There are four steps to solve for a single unknown variable:

1. Set up the equation
2. Simplify both sides of the equation
3. Get the variable on one side
4. Isolate the variable

Example #1: Solve for x in this equation:

$4x + 30 − 20 + 8x = x + 100 + 20 + x$

Since we have an equation already, we will first simplify both sides of the equation by adding all of the like terms. We'll add all of the x's together and all of the numbers together.

$12x + 10 = 2x + 120$

Next, we need to get all the x's on one side. To do this, we can subtract 2x from both sides of the equation so that all the x's are on the left side.

$10x + 10 = 120$

Afterwards, we need to isolate the x. To do this, we can subtract 10 from both sides of the equation and then divide both sides of the equation by 10.

$10x = 110$

$x = 11$

Let's take a look at another example.

Example #2: $-8x + 2x - 10 + 11 = 14 - 4x + 8 + x$

$-6x + 1 = 22 - 3x$

$-3x + 1 = 22$

$-3x = 21$

$x = -7$

How to Solve for Two Unknown Variables

Sometimes, a case interview problem will give you two equations with two unknown variables to solve for. This requires a bit more work, but follows a lot of the same principles as solving for a single unknown variable.

It's important to know that if you have two unknown variables that you are simultaneously trying to solve for, you must have two different equations. If you don't, it will be impossible to solve for.

There are two different ways to solve for two unknown variables:

- Substitution method
- Elimination method

Substitution method

There are four steps to using the substitution method:

1. Solve for one variable in terms of the other variable in one equation
2. Substitute that into the other equation
3. Solve for the first unknown variable
4. Solve for the second unknown variable using the first solved variable

Let's walk through an example to illustrate this.

Example: Solve for x and y in these equations:

1) $x + y = 100$

2) $30x + 50y = 4{,}000$

The first step is to solve for one variable in terms of the other. We can pick either equation to do this. Let's pick the first equation since it is simpler.

We can also choose to solve for either variable first. Let's start with x first.

$x = 100 - y$

Next, we'll plug this into the other equation that we haven't used yet.

$30 * (100 - y) + 50y = 4{,}000$

Now, we can solve for the first unknown variable.

$3{,}000 - 30y + 50y = 4{,}000$

$20y = 1{,}000$

$y = 50$

Lastly, we need to solve for the second unknown variable. We can do this by plugging in the value of y into either equation. Let's do this for the first equation since that one is simpler.

$x + (50) = 100$

$x = 50$

At this point, we've solved for both variables, $x = 50$ and $y = 50$.

Let's take a look at the second method of solving for two unknown variables.

Elimination method

There are four steps to using the elimination method to solve for two variables:

1. Align both equations
2. Add or subtract the equations to eliminate one variable
3. Solve for the remaining variable
4. Substitute the solved variable to solve for the other variable

Let's walk through an example to illustrate this.

Example: Solve for x and y in these equations:

1) $2x + 3y = 18$

2) $-6y - 12 = -8x$

Let's first align both equations so that the variables and constants line up vertically. Let's keep the first equation the same, but rearrange the terms in the second equation.

1) $2x + 3y = 18$

2) $8x - 6y = 12$

Now that the equations are aligned, we need to add or subtract the equations to eliminate one variable. Let's try to eliminate the y's first.

To do this, we need to multiply the first equation by 2.

1) $4x + 6y = 36$

2) $8x - 6y = 12$

Now, we can add both equations to get rid of the y's.

$12x = 48$

The next step is to solve for x.

$x = 4$

Now that we know x, we can solve for y by plugging in the value of x into either equation. Let's do this for the first equation.

$2(4) + 3y = 18$

$8 + 3y = 18$

$3y = 10$

$y = 10/3$

At this point, we've solved for both variables, $x = 4$ and $y = 10/3$.

Summary

- Algebra is a way of solving problems by using letters to stand for unknown numbers and then figuring out what those numbers are

- A variable is just a symbol, usually a letter such as x, that stands for a number that you don't know

- There are four steps to solve for a single unknown variable:

    o Set up the equation

    o Simplify both sides of the equation

    o Get the variable on one side

    o Isolate the variable

- To solve for two unknown variables, you must have two different equations and can use either the substitution method or the elimination method

- Substitution method:

    o Solve for one variable in terms of the other variable in one equation

    o Substitute that into the other equation

    o Solve for the first unknown variable

    o Solve for the second unknown variable using the first solved variable

- Elimination method:

    o Align both equations

- Add or subtract the equations to eliminate one variable

- Solve for the remaining variable

- Substitute the solved variable to solve for the other variable

Practice Problems

Solve for the unknown variable or variables in the following equations.

1. $(3x + 5)/2 = 10$

2. $5(x-2) + 3x = 46$

3. $(4x-6)/3 + (x+2)/2 = 10$

4. $(5x-10)/2 = 3x+2$

5. $(x+1)/4 + (x-2)/2 = 9$

6. $2x + 3y = 24$

   $x - y = 2$

7. $4x - y = 15$

   $4x + 2y = 30$

8. $2x + 4y = 34$

   $3x + 5y = 41$

9. $5x + 3y = 41$

   $2x - y = 1$

10. $7x - 2y = 12$

    $x + 16y = 18$

Solutions

1. $x = 5$
2. $x = 7$
3. $x = 6$
4. $x = -14$
5. $x = 13$
6. $x = 6, y = 4$
7. $x = 5, y = 5$
8. $x = -3, y = 10$
9. $x = 4, y = 7$
10. $x = 2, y = 1$

9. Profit Formulas

Why Profit Formulas Matter

Profit questions are one of the most common types of quantitative problems you'll be given in a case interview.

Whether you're analyzing a declining business, launching a new product, or evaluating a pricing strategy, understanding profit helps you answer the core question: is this making money?

The formulas for profit are simple, but the application of the formulas can get quite complex. So, make sure you fully understand every single equation in this chapter.

These equations shouldn't feel like something you are forced to memorize. Instead, these equations should feel intuitive.

Profit

Profit is the amount of money a business earns after taking into account costs. The basic formula for profit is:

Profit = Revenue – Costs

Revenue is the amount of money a business receives from selling its products or services.

Cost is the amount of money a business spends to make and deliver its products or services.

Example #1: A company generated $5M in revenue last year and had $2M in costs. What was its profit?

Profit = Revenue – Cost

Profit = $5M - $2M

Profit = $3M

The basic formula for revenue is:

Revenue = Quantity * Price

Quantity refers to the number of units of a product or service sold. Price is the amount of money charged for one unit of a product or service.

Example #2: A company sold 10,000 units of a product last year that was priced at $20. What was its revenue?

Revenue = Quantity * Price

Revenue = 10,000 * $20

Revenue = $200,000

This is not the only way to calculate revenue. If a company has multiple products, the formula for revenue becomes:

Revenue = Revenue of Product A + Revenue of Product B + …

Or in other words:

Revenue = (Quantity$_A$ * Price$_A$) + (Quantity$_B$ * Price$_B$) + ...

If a company sells in multiple regions, then the formula for revenue could look like:

Revenue = Revenue in Country A + Revenue in Country B + ...

Example #3: A company sells its products in two countries. In Country A, the company sold 100,000 units at a price of $3 per unit. In Country B, the company sold 400,000 units at a price of $2 per unit. What is the company's total revenue?

Revenue = (Quantity$_A$ * Price$_A$) + (Quantity$_B$ * Price$_B$)

Revenue = (100,000 * $3) + (400,000 * $2)

Revenue = $1,100,000

While the exact formula for revenue depends on the specific case interview problem you are given, all you need to know fundamentally is that revenue is the product of quantity and price.

Costs are comprised of two components: variable costs and fixed costs.

Costs = Total Variable Costs + Fixed Costs

Variable costs are costs that change depending on how many products or services a business makes or sells.

Examples of variable costs include:

- Raw materials
- Packaging
- Shipping costs
- Sales commissions

As a company makes more products, these costs directly increase. For each new unit that is made, companies will have to pay more for each of these variable costs.

Total variable costs can be calculated using the formula:

Total Variable Costs = Quantity * Variable Cost

In other words, the total variable cost is calculated by multiplying the number of units produced times the variable cost per unit.

Fixed costs are costs that stay the same no matter how much a business makes or sells.

Examples of fixed costs include:

- Rent
- Equipment
- Salaries
- Insurance
- Property taxes
- Loan payments

Example #4: A company sold 20,000 units of a product last year. Each product has a variable cost of $300. The company also has annual fixed costs of $5M. What was the company's total costs?

Costs = Total Variable Costs + Fixed Costs

Costs = (Quantity * Variable Cost) + Fixed Costs

Costs = (20,000 * $300) + $5M

Costs = $11M

Putting all of these formulas together, we can expand our original basic formula for profit:

Profit = Revenue − Cost

Profit = (Quantity * Price) − (Total Variable Costs + Fixed Costs)

Profit = (Quantity * Price) − [(Quantity * Variable Cost) + Fixed Costs]

We can rearrange some of these terms to get the following formula:

Profit = (Price − Variable Cost) * Quantity − Fixed Costs

This is another helpful and intuitive way to think about profit.

"Price − Variable Cost" gives you the profit per unit sold. After multiplying this by the quantity of units sold, this gives you the profit before accounting for fixed cost.

After subtracting fixed costs, this gets you the actual profit for the company.

There is one more thing you need to know about this profit formula. "Price − Variable Cost" is sometimes referred to as the contribution margin.

Contribution Margin = Price − Variable Cost

Contribution margin is the amount of money left from sales after subtracting variable costs. It contributes to covering fixed costs and generating profit for the company.

Example #5: A company's product has a contribution margin of $100. It sold 200,000 units last year and had $15M in annual fixed costs. What were the company's profits?

Profit = (Price − Variable Cost) * Quantity − Fixed Costs

Profit = Contribution Margin * Quantity − Fixed Costs

Profit = ($100 * 200,000) - $15M

Profit = $5M

Profit Margin

Next, we'll discuss profit margin. While profit margin and profit sound like the same thing, they are very different.

Profit is the amount of money a business earns after taking into account costs.

Profit margin is the percentage of each sale that a company keeps as profit after covering all costs.

So, remember that profit is measured in a currency, such as dollars. Profit margin, on the other hand, is measured as a percentage.

The formula for profit margin is quite simple:

Profit Margin = Profit / Revenue

It can also be re-written as:

Profit Margin = (Revenue − Costs) / Revenue

Example #1: A company made $4,000 in profit on $20,000 in revenue. What is its profit margin?

Profit Margin = Profit / Revenue

Profit Margin = $4,000 / $20,000

Profit Margin = 20%

Let's take a look at another example.

Example #2: A company has sold 400,000 units of a product at $25. Each unit has a variable cost of $20. The company incurs $1.2M in fixed costs per year. What is the company's profit margin?

Profit = (Price − Variable Cost) * Quantity − Fixed Costs

Profit = ($25 − $20) * 400,000 − $1.2M

Profit = $800,000

Revenue = 400,000 * $25

Revenue = $10,000,000

Profit Margin = Profit / Revenue

Profit Margin = $800,000 / $10,000,000

Profit Margin = 8%

Breakeven Point

Breakeven is when a business earns just enough revenue to cover its total costs. In other words, the business has no profits or losses.

Breakeven analysis is typically used when evaluating new product launches, deciding whether to enter a new market, or determining pricing strategies.

The basic formula for breakeven is: Profit = 0

If we expand upon the various formulas for profit, we get the following formula:

(Price − Variable Cost) * Quantity = Fixed Costs

Example #1: A company has $5,000 in fixed costs. Each product the company sells is priced at $25 and has a variable cost of $15. How many units does the company need to sell to cover its costs?

(Price − Variable Cost) * Quantity = Fixed Costs

($25 − $15) * Quantity = $5,000

Quantity = 500

The company has to sell 500 units to break even.

Let's take a look at another example.

Example #2: A company is launching a new product and expects to sell 4,000 units per year. The annual fixed costs are $100,000. The variable cost per unit is $25. What is the minimum price the product should be set at in order to break even?

(Price − Variable Cost) * Quantity = Fixed Costs

(Price − $25) * 4,000 = $100,000

Price = $50

The product needs to be priced at $50 to break even.

Summary

- Profit is the amount of money a business earns after taking into account costs

- Profit = Revenue − Costs

- Revenue = Quantity * Price

- Costs = Total Variable Costs + Fixed Costs

- Total Variable Costs = Quantity * Variable Cost

- Profit = (Price − Variable Cost) * Quantity − Fixed Costs

- Contribution Margin = Price − Variable Cost

- Profit margin is the percentage of each sale that a company keeps as profit after covering all costs

- Profit Margin = Profit / Revenue

- Breakeven is when a business earns just enough revenue to cover its total costs, when the business has no profits or losses

Practice Problems

1. A company manufactures two types of laptops. Standard models sell for $1,000 each and cost $900 to produce. Premium models sell for $2,000 each and cost $1,200 to produce.

   The company sells 4 standard models for every 1 premium model. What is the average percent profit margin per laptop sold?

2. In the previous problem, how many total laptops must be sold in a month to break even if fixed costs are $240,000 per month?

3. A company is launching a new tech gadget that has a production cost of $90. They'd like to have a gross profit margin of 40%. After production, distribution and packaging adds another $15 in costs per unit.

   What should the price be to meet the margin target?

4. A company sells 15,000 units at $50 each. The total fixed costs are $120,000. Their variable costs per unit is $40.

   Next year, fixed costs will increase by $30,000. At the same time, variable costs will increase by 10% per unit due to supplier issues.

   By what absolute number of units must sales increase to maintain total profit?

5. In the previous problem, if they keep selling only 15,000 units, what is the drop in profit?

6. A consulting firm has two services. Strategy projects are billed at $250/hour at a 60% margin. Operations projects are billed at $150/hour at a 40% margin.

The expected work mix is 70% strategy and 30% operations. What is the average margin across the business?

7. In the previous problem, how many hours must be billed annually to break even if annual fixed costs are $615,000?

8. This year, a company sold 100,000 units at a price of $50 per unit and a cost per unit of $30.

    Next year, the units sold is expected to drop by 20%, prices are expected to drop by 8%, and costs are expected to increase by 20%.

    How much will total profits decrease by in dollars?

9. In the previous problem, what percentage of the decrease in profit is attributable to each of the three factors?

Solutions

1. **20%**

    To calculate the average percent profit margin per laptop, we need to calculate the average revenue and average profit.

    Average revenue = [(4 * $1,000) + (1 * $2,000)]/5 = $1,200

    Profit per standard laptop = $1,000 - $900 = $100

    Profit per premium laptop = $2,000 - $1,200 = $800

    Average profit = [(4 * $100) + (1 * $800)]/5 = $240

    Average profit margin = $240/$1,200 = 20%

2. **1,000**

    We have the average profit per laptop from the previous question. To calculate the breakeven point, we can just divide fixed costs by this number.

    Breakeven = $240,000 fixed costs / $240 profit per laptop = 1,000 units

3. **$175**

    Costs = $90 + $15 = $105

    Price = $105 / (1 – 40%)

    Price = $175

4. **15,000 more units need to be sold**

    Let's calculate the current profit.

    Profit = 15,000 * ($50 - $40) - $120,000 = $30,000

Let's calculate the new fixed costs and variable costs.

New Fixed Cost = $120,000 + $30,000 = $150,000

New Variable Cost = $40 * (1 + 10%) = $44

Next, we can set up an equation and solve for the number of units that need to be sold to maintain the same profit.

$30,000 = ($50 - $44) * Quantity - $150,000

Quantity = 30,000 units

So, the company needs to sell 30,000 units, an increase of 15,000 units over what it currently sells.

5. **Profit decreases by $90,000**

   Let's calculate the profit if the quantity sold is unchanged.

   Profit = ($50 - $44) * 15,000 - $150,000 = -$60,000

   Profit decreases from $30,000 to -$60,000. So, profit decreases by $90,000.

6. **54%**

   Average Profit Margin = (70% * 60%) + (30% * 40%) = 54%

7. **5,000 hours**

   Profit per hour of strategy projects = $250 * 60% = $150

   Profit per hour of operations projects = $150 * 40% = $60

   Average profit per hour = (70% * $150) + (30% * $60) = $123

   Breakeven = $615,000 / $123 per hour = 5,000 hours

8. **Profits will decrease by $1,200,000**

Current Profit = 100,000 * ($50 - $30) = $2,000,000

New Volume = 100,000 * (1 - 20%) = 80,000

New Price = $50 * (1 - 8%) = $46

New Cost Per Unit = $30 * (1 + 20%) = $36

New Profit = 80,000 * ($46 - $36) = $800,000

Change in Profit = $800,000 - $2,000,000 = -$1,200,000

9. **~29% due to volume, ~29% due to price, ~42% due to costs**

    To find the percentage attributable to each factor, calculate the drop in profit for each factor assuming no other factors change.

    New Profit if Only Volume Changes = 80,000 * ($50 - $30) = $1,600,000

    Change in Profit Due to Drop in Volume = $1,600,000 - $2,000,000 = -$400,000

    New Profit if Only Price Changes = 100,000 * ($46 - $30) = $1,600,000

    Change in Profit Due to Drop in Price = $1,600,000 - $2,000,000 = -$400,000

    New Profit if Only Costs Change = 100,000 * ($50 - $36) = $1,400,000

    Change in Profit Due to Increase in Costs = $1,400,000 - $2,000,000 = -$600,000

    Only changing quantity causes profit to decrease by $400,000, only changing price causes profit to decrease by $400,000, and only changing costs causes profit to decrease by $600,000.

Therefore, the ratio of each factor's impact is 2:2:3. Converting this to a percentage gives us our answer.

10. Investment Formulas

Why Investment Formulas Matter

In some case interviews, you'll be asked to evaluate whether an investment is worth it. This could be a new product, a marketing campaign, an acquisition or expanding to a new region.

To answer these questions, you'll need to quickly and confidently use two key investment math formulas:

- Return on investment

- Payback period

These formulas help assess whether an investment creates value, how quickly it returns money, and whether it's a good use of capital.

There are other investment formulas that are a lot more complicated. However, those formulas are almost never used in a case interview.

Remember, you don't need any technical knowledge to succeed in a case interview. These are the only two formulas you need to know.

Return on Investment

Return on investment, or ROI for short, measures how much profit or value is generated from an investment compared to the money that was initially invested.

This is the most commonly used metric for assessing investments in case interviews.

ROI = Profit / Initial Investment

ROI is typically expressed as a percentage. So, after doing the calculations, you should convert the resulting number to a percentage.

Example #1: A company spends $200,000 on a marketing campaign. The campaign generates $750,000 in revenue and has $500,000 in costs associated with delivering those sales. What is the ROI?

ROI = Profit / Initial Investment

ROI = ($750,000 - $500,000 - $200,000) / $200,000

ROI = $50,000 / $200,000

ROI = 25%

Let's take a look at another example.

Example #2: A hotel chain spends $730,000 to renovate one of its properties, updating rooms, improving amenities, and remodeling the lobby. As a result, the hotel is able to:

- Increase its average room rate by $30 per night
- Maintain an average occupancy of 100 rooms per night
- Continue to operate 365 days a year

What is the ROI of making this change in the first year?

First, let's calculate the increase in profit.

Profit = $30 * 100 * 365 - $730,000

Profit = $365,000

ROI = Profit / Initial Investment

ROI = $365,000 / $730,000

ROI = 50%

Payback Period

Payback period tells you how long it takes for an investment to repay itself. In other words, how long it takes for an investment to break even.

Payback Period = Initial Investment / Profit Per Year

Example #1: A company spends $1,000,000 to install energy-efficient equipment. This installation saves $250,000 per year in utility bills. What is the payback period of this investment?

Payback Period = Initial Investment / Profit Per Year

Payback Period = $1,000,000 / $250,000

Payback Period = 4

It will take 4 years to recoup the investment.

Let's take a look at another example.

Example #2: A logistics company spends $1.2M on robotic automation equipment for a warehouse. The investment is expected to generate:

- $100,000 in savings in year 1

- $200,000 in savings in year 2

- $300,000 in savings in year 3

- $400,000 in savings in year 4

- $500,000 in savings in year 5

What is the payback period?

Since the savings each year is not the same for each year, we can't simply divide the initial investment by the annual savings.

Instead, we need to figure out when the total cumulative savings reaches $1.2M, the initial cost of the investment.

After 4 years, the total cumulative savings is $1M.

After 5 years, the total cumulative savings is $1.5M.

So, we know that the payback period is somewhere between year 4 and year 5.

To estimate where in between these two years, we'll have to assume that the savings is spread out evenly throughout each year.

So, after 4 years, the total cumulative savings is $1M and we need another $200K in savings to break even.

We know that year 5 has a total of $500K in savings. If we divide $200K by $500K, we get 0.4.

So, the payback period is roughly 4.4 years.

Summary

- Return on investment, or ROI for short, measures how much profit or value is generated from an investment compared to the money that was initially invested

- ROI = Net Profit / Initial Investment

- Payback period tells you how long it takes for an investment to repay itself or to break even

- Payback Period = Initial Investment / Profit Per Year

Practice Problems

1. A company is considering launching a new product and has made the following projections:

   The initial investment required for the product launch is $2,000,000.

   The projected revenue in the first 5 years is: $500,000, $800,000, $1,200,000, $1,500,000, and $1,800,000.

   The product's operating costs, including labor, materials, and marketing, are projected to be 50% of the revenue each year.

   What is the ROI over the first 5 years?

2. In the previous problem, what is the payback period?

3. A company is considering investing in a new software product that will generate $15,000,000 in cash flow over the next 5 years. Assume there are no costs to maintain the software. The company expects to sell the software product for $7,500,000 at the end of Year 5.

   If the company wants an ROI of at least 50% over this 5-year period, what is the maximum they can invest in this product?

4. A company is evaluating an investment in a new technology that will help increase its manufacturing efficiency. The initial investment required to implement the technology is $8,000,000. At the end of 4 years, the company expects to sell the technology for $4,000,000.

   If the company desires an ROI of 60% over the next 4 years, how much manufacturing savings should the technology generate over this period?

Solutions

1. **45%**

   Revenue = $500,000 + $800,000 + $1,200,000 + $1,500,000 + $1,800,000 = $5,800,000

   Profit = 50% * $5,800,000 - $2,000,000 = $900,000

   ROI = 900,000 / $2,000,000 = 45%

2. **4 years**

   The profit in each of the first five years is: $250,000, $400,000, $600,000, $750,000, and $900,000.

   After 4 years, the total profit is $2,000,000, which equals the initial investment. Therefore, the payback period is 4 years.

3. **$15,000,000**

   Net Profit = $15,000,000 + $7,500,000 − Initial Investment

   ROI = Net Profit / Initial Investment

   0.50 = ($22,500,000 − Initial Investment)/ Initial Investment

   Initial Investment * 1.5 = $22,500,000

   Initial Investment = $15,000,000

4. **$8,800,000**

   ROI = Net Profit / Initial Investment

   Net Profit = $8,000,000 * 60% = $4,800,000

   $4,800,000 = Manufacturing Savings + $4,000,000 - $8,000,000

   Manufacturing Savings = $8,800,000

11. Operations Formulas

Why Operations Formulas Matter

In case interviews, you may be asked to analyze and improve a company's operational efficiency. You may be tasked with identifying operational bottlenecks or opportunities for efficiency improvements.

Understanding key operations formulas will help you quantify performance and make data-driven recommendations.

The formulas in this chapter will provide the foundation for assessing a variety of different manufacturing and logistics processes.

Remember, you don't need to have any technical knowledge or experience related to manufacturing or operations. You only need to be familiar with a few basic formulas.

Output

In operations, output refers to the amount of work produced by something in a given time period. This can be a machine, person, factory, or process.

Output = Rate * Time

This formula has various versions that apply to many different situations.

- Units Produced = Production Rate * Time

- Labor Hours = Hours Worked per Worker * Workers

- Work = Rate * Time

- Distance = Speed * Time

Example #1: A factory can produce 150 units of a product in an hour. How many units can it produce in a 24-hour day?

Output = Rate * Time

Output = 150 units per hour * 24 hours

Output = 3,600 units

Let's take a look at another example.

Example #2: A company runs a factory that produces custom packaging boxes. Currently, 3 machines each run 8 hours per day. Each machine produces 20 boxes per hour. The company wants to increase daily production by 50% to meet rising customer demand.

There are new machines available for purchase that can produce 30 boxes per hour. How many new machines should the client add, assuming each machine still runs 8 hours per day?

Current Output = Rate * Time

Current Output = 3 machines * 20 boxes per hour * 8 hours per day

Current Output = 480 boxes per day

Increasing daily production by 50% means producing an additional 240 boxes per day.

240 boxes per day = Number of Machines * 30 boxes per hour * 8 hours per day

Number of Machines = 1

The company needs to add 1 new machine to meet the rising customer demand.

Utilization

Utilization measures how efficiently something is being used relative to its potential. This can apply to many different things, such as machines, equipment, and labor.

In other words, it's the ratio of the actual usage to maximum possible usage.

Utilization = Actual Output / Maximum Possible Output

Utilization is typically expressed as a percentage. So, after making calculations, convert the resulting number to a percentage.

Low utilization indicates inefficiencies. There may be idle time, machine breakdowns, or misaligned capacity.

High utilization is often good, but beware of pushing resources too hard. This can lead to breakdowns, lower quality, or burnout.

Example #1: A packaging machine is capable of producing 200 units per hour. However, over the course of a shift, it only produces 150 units per hour. What is the machine's utilization?

Utilization = Actual Output / Maximum Possible Output

Utilization = 150 / 200

Utilization = 75%

Let's take a look at another example.

Example #2: A local hospital has 4 MRI machines, each available 12 hours per day. The average scan takes 45 minutes, which includes setup and cleanup. On a typical day, the hospital conducts 32 MRI scans total.

What is the utilization rate of these machines?

Maximum Output = 4 machines * 12 hours per day * 60 minutes per day / 45 minutes per scan

Maximum Output = 64 scans

Utilization = Actual Output / Maximum Possible Output

Utilization = 32 scans / 64 scans

Utilization = 50%

Summary

- Output refers to the amount of work produced by something in a given period of time (e.g., machine, person, factory, process)

- Output = Rate * Time

- Utilization measures how efficiently something is being used relative to its potential, the ratio of actual usage to maximum possible usage

- Utilization = Actual Output / Maximum Possible Output

Practice Problems

1. A manufacturing company is preparing for an 8-week production run. The company needs to achieve a total of 18,000 labor hours over this time period.

   They have 45 full-time workers that are scheduled to work 40 hours per week. Additional temporary workers can be contracted, but can only work 30 hours per week.

   How many temporary workers must the company hire to meet the labor hour requirement?

2. A manufacturing plant operates three machines in parallel, each with the following conditions.

   Machine A: Produces 300 units per hour, but has 20% downtime each day due to maintenance.

   Machine B: Produces 450 units per hour, but experiences 5% downtime each day due to occasional malfunctions.

   Machine C: Produces 500 units per hour, but operates for 7 hours a day due to shortages in staff, whereas the other machines operate for 10 hours.

   What is the total actual output for the day across all three machines?

3. In the previous problem, what is the overall utilization of the manufacturing plant?

4. A factory is producing customized furniture sets. It operates two shifts per day. Each shift is 8 hours long, but each shift also has a mandatory 1-hour break that reduces effective working time.

   Last month the factory produced 3,360 furniture sets while operating for 25 days.

Due to material shortages, for 20% of the time, the machines were operating at 80% of their regular rate.

What is the regular production rate under full operating conditions?

5. A delivery company sends a truck to deliver packages between two cities that are 400 miles apart.

   For the first 60% of the distance, the truck travels at an average speed of 45 miles per hour due to heavy traffic.

   For the remaining 40% of the trip, the traffic clears and the truck speeds up to 75 miles per hour.

   The driver also has a mandatory 30-minute break after driving 200 miles.

   What is the total time it takes the truck to complete a one-way trip?

6. A construction company is tasked with building a large office complex. The project consists of three phases: Foundation (120 tasks), Structure (180 tasks), and Finishing (100 tasks).

   The company hires two teams to complete the entire project. Team A is responsible for the Foundation and Structure phases. Team B is responsible for the Finishing phase.

   If Team B is expected to finish in 10 weeks and Team A works 50% faster than Team B, how long will Team A take to finish the phases they are responsible for?

Solutions

1. **15 temporary workers**

    Full-time worker labor hours = 45 * 40 * 8 = 14,400 hours

    Remaining labor hours needed = 18,000 − 14,400 = 3,600

    Temporary workers needed = 3,600 / (8 * 30) = 15

2. **10,175 units**

    Machine A output = 10 * (1 − 20%) * 300 = 2,400 units

    Machine B output = 10 * (1 − 5%) * 450 = 4,275 units

    Machine C output = 7 * 500 = 3,500 units

    Total output = 2,400 + 4,275 + 3,500 = 10,175 units

3. **81.4%**

    Maximum output = 10 * (300 + 450 + 500) = 12,500

    Utilization = 10,175 / 12,500 = 81.4%

4. **10 units per hour**

    Total working hours in the month = 25 days * 2 shifts * (8 − 1 hours per shift) = 350 hours

    Let R = regular production rate

    3,360 = (80% * 350 * R) + (20% * 350 * 0.8 * R)

    3,360 = 280R + 56R

    R = 10 units per hour

5. **7 hours 58 min**

Distance of first segment = 60% * 400 = 240 miles

Distance of second segment = 40% * 400 = 160 miles

Time of first segment = 240 / 45 = 16 / 3 = 5 hours 20 min

Time of second segment = 160 / 75 = 32 / 15 = 2 hours 8 min

Break time = 30 min

Total travel time = 5 hours 20 min + 2 hours 8 min + 30 min = 7 hours 58 min

6. **20 weeks**

    Team B rate = 100 tasks / 10 weeks = 10 tasks per week

    Team A rate = 1.5 * 10 tasks per week = 15 tasks per week

    Team A time = (120 + 180) / 15 = 20 weeks

12. Market Share Formulas

Why Market Share Formulas Matter

In case interviews, you'll often be asked to evaluate a company's competitive position. One of the most common and powerful ways to do this is by calculating market share.

Understanding a company's market share helps answer questions such as:

- How big is this player compared to its competitors?
- What's the potential for growth in this market?
- How fragmented or concentrated is the industry?

This chapter covers the two most important formulas you need to know:

- Market share
- Relative market share

Market Share

Market share measures the percentage of total market sales a particular company has. It's a straightforward way to understand how dominant or small a company is within a given industry.

Market shares can range from 0%, no presence in the market, to 100%, complete dominance in the market.

The formula for market share is:

Market Share = Company Revenue / Total Market Revenue

This is the most common way of calculating market share. However, you should know that market share can also be calculated by using units sold or volume instead of revenue.

Example #1: A client in the packaged snacks industry wants to understand how they stack up against competitors. They generated $400M in sales last year while the total market for packaged snacks was $10B. What is their market share?

Market Share = Company Revenue / Total Market Revenue

Market Share = $400M / $10B

Market Share = 4%

This company has a small presence in the packaged snacks market.

Let's take a look at another example.

Example #2: A beverage company sells two main products: bottled water and iced tea. They want to understand their total market share in the non-carbonated beverage market. Assume there are no other types of drinks in the non-carbonated beverage market.

You are given the following data points:

- The company sells 5M units of bottled water at an average price of $1 per unit

- The company sells 1.5M units of iced tea at an average price of $2 per unit

- The entire bottled water market is 400M units with an average price of $0.75 per unit

- The entire iced tea market is 200M units with an average price of $2.50 per unit

Company Revenue = (5M * $1) + (1.5M * $2) = $8M

Total Market Revenue = (400M * $0.75) + (200M * $2.50) = $800M

Market Share = $8M / $800M = 1%

The company has a 1% market share in the non-carbonated beverage market.

Relative Market Share

While absolute market share shows a company's size compared to the total market, relative market share compares it directly to its largest competitor.

This is helpful for telling you how strong a company is relative to the industry leader.

Here's the formula for relative market share:

Relative Market Share = Company Market Share / Market Share of Largest Competitor

It can also be calculated by using revenue.

Relative Market Share = Company Revenue / Revenue of Largest Competitor

Relative market share is typically expressed as a number. Here's how to interpret relative market shares:

- A relative market share that is less than 1 indicates that the company is not the market leader

- A relative market share of exactly 1 indicates that the company is tied with their largest competitor

- A relative market share greater than 1 indicates market leadership

Example #1: Your client has 10% market share. The market leader has 20% market share. What is your client's relative market share?

Relative Market Share = Company Market Share / Market Share of Largest Competitor

Relative Market Share = 10% / 20%

Relative Market Share = 0.5

Your client's relative market share is 0.5. In other words, they have half the market share of the market leader.

Let's take a look at another example.

Example #2: Your client had $600M in frozen food sales last year. Their largest competitor has 20% market share. The total market size for frozen food is $2.4B. What is your client's relative market share?

Client Market Share = $600M / $2.4B = 25%

Relative Market Share = 25% / 20%

Relative Market Share = 1.25

Your client's relative market share is 1.25. In other words, they have 25% higher market share than the next largest competitor.

Summary

- Market share measures the percentage of total market sales a particular company has, ranging from 0% to 100%

- Market Share = Company Revenue / Total Market Revenue

- There are two ways to calculate relative market share:

    o Relative Market Share = Company Market Share / Market Share of Largest Competitor

    o Relative Market Share = Company Revenue / Revenue of Largest Competitor

- How to interpret relative market shares:

    o A relative market share that is less than 1 indicates that the company is not the market leader

    o A relative market share of exactly 1 indicates that the company is tied with their largest competitor

    o A relative market share greater than 1 indicates market leadership

Practice Problems

1. The electric vehicle market size last year was $100B. It is expected to grow by 20% this year.

   Last year, your client had electric vehicle sales of $1.5B. However, due to significant investments in marketing and new innovations, they are expected to increase sales by 50% this year.

   The largest competitor in the market had sales of $24B. They are expected to increase sales by 25% this year.

   What is your client's expected market share this year?

2. Based on the previous problem, what is your client's expected relative market share this year?

3. The global solar panel market has a total market size of $500B this year. The key players and their relative market share are as follows:

   SolarTech has a relative market share of 0.25 compared to SunPower.

   SunPower generated $120B in revenue this year.

   RadiantGrid entered the market a few years ago and holds 12% of the total market share this year.

   What is SolarTech's relative market share compared to RadiantGrid?

4. The total laptop market this year is $500B and consists of three players. Player A is twice as large as Player B. Player C's revenue is $50B less than Player A.

   What are the market shares of each player?

Solutions

1. **1.875%**

    Market size this year = $100B * 1.2 = $120B

    Client sales this year = $1.5B * 1.5 = $2.25B

    Market share this year = $2.25B / $120B = 1.875%

2. **0.075**

    Largest competitor's sales this year = $24B * 1.25 = $30B

    Largest competitor's market share this year = $30B / $120B = 25%

    Client's relative market share this year = 1.875% / 25% = 0.075

3. **0.5**

    SolarTech revenue = 0.25 * $120B = $30B

    SolarTech market share = $30B / $500B = 6%

    SolarTech relative market share = 6% / 12% = 0.5

4. **Player A = 44%, Player B = 22%, Player C = 34%**

    Player B revenue = x

    Player A revenue = 2x

    Player C revenue = 2x − 50

    x + 2x + 2x − 50 = 500

    5x = 550

$x = 110$

Player A market share = 2 * 110 / 500 = 44%

Player B market share = 110 / 500 = 22%

Player C market share = (2 * 110 − 50) / 500 = 34%

13. Finance Formulas

Why Finance Formulas Matter

Some basic finance formulas show up in many consulting case interviews, especially when analyzing a company's performance or evaluating potential investments.

The good news is that most finance formulas used in case interviews are very simple.

You just need to understand how to calculate specific financial numbers and how to interpret them to better understand businesses.

In this chapter, we'll break down key finance formulas you may need to use in case interviews in plain, simple language. So, don't worry if you don't have a finance background, we'll teach you everything you need to know.

Gross Profit

Gross profit is how much money a company makes after covering the direct costs of producing its product or service.

These direct costs are known as COGS, which stands for Cost of Goods Sold.

While there are some technical distinctions between COGS and variable costs, you can effectively think of them as the same thing for the purpose of solving case interviews.

Gross Profit = Revenue – COGS

Gross margin tells you what percentage of revenue remains after taking into account COGS. This is a helpful metric for comparing performance over time or between companies.

Gross Margin = Gross Profit / Revenue

Let's take a look at some examples to illustrate these formulas.

Example #1: Your client sells $2 million worth of clothing. It costs them $1.4 million to manufacture the clothes. What is the gross profit and gross margin?

Gross Profit = Revenue – COGS

Gross Profit = $2M - $1.4M = $600K

Gross Margin = Gross Profit / Revenue

Gross Margin = $600K / $2M = 30%

The gross profit is $600K and the gross margin is 30%.

Let's take a look at another example.

Example #2: A bakery chain sells two main product lines: cakes and cookies. They sold 20,000 cakes at $25 each and 100,000 cookies at $2 each. The cost to produce one cake is $10 and the cost to produce one cookie is $0.50. What is their gross profit?

Revenue = (20,000 * $25) + (100,000 * $2)

Revenue = $700,000

COGS = (20,000 * $10) + (100,000 * $0.50) = $250,000

Gross Profit = Revenue - COGS

Gross Profit = $700,000 - $250,000 = $450,000

The bakery's gross profit is $450,000.

Operating Profit

Operating profit is the profit a company makes after covering both the direct and indirect costs of producing its product or service.

To calculate operating profit, start with gross profit and subtract any operating expenses.

Operating Profit = Gross Profit - Operating Expenses

For the purpose of solving case interviews, you can think of operating expenses as fixed costs even though there are some technical differences between the two.

Operating expenses includes things such as:

- Salaries and wages
- Rent and utilities
- Marketing and advertising
- Office supplies
- Depreciation
- Amortization

- Insurance

- Professional services

- Repairs and maintenance

Two operating expenses that you might not be familiar with are depreciation and amortization. These are expenses that help account for how assets lose value over time.

Depreciation applies to tangible assets or things that you can physically touch. Tangible assets include equipment, vehicles, and buildings.

Since these assets wear out or become outdated, depreciation spreads the cost of them over their useful life.

Amortization is similar, but applies to intangible assets or things you can't physically touch. Intangible assets include patents, trademarks, and software licenses.

Amortization is a way to spread the cost of these assets over their useful life.

Operating margin tells you what percentage of revenue becomes operating profit. This is another helpful metric for comparing performance over time or between companies.

Operating Margin = Operating Profit / Revenue

Let's take a look at some examples to illustrate these formulas.

Example #1: A company has $10M in revenue, $5M in COGS, $2.5M of marketing, $1M of depreciation, and $500K of amortization. What is the company's operating profit and operating margin?

Operating Profit = Gross Profit – Operating Expenses

Operating Profit = Revenue – COGS – Operating Expenses

Operating Profit = $10M - $5M - ($2.5M + $1M + $500K) = $1M

Operating Margin = Operating Profit / Revenue

Operating Margin = $1M / $10M = 10%

The operating profit is $1M and the operating margin is 10%.

Let's take a look at another example.

Example #2: A movie theater had 500,000 visitors last year. The average ticket price was $12 and the average concession sale per visitor was $5. The cost to serve each visitor is $7.50 per person.

The company also spent $300,000 on advertising, $150,000 on corporate overhead allocations, and $250,000 in rent. The theater depreciates its equipment at $100,000 per year and amortizes lease improvements at $50,000 per year. What is their operating profit?

Revenue = 500,000 * ($12 + $5) = $8.5M

COGS = 500,000 * $7.50 = $3.75M

Gross Profit = $8.5M - $3.75M = $4.75M

Operating Expenses = $300K + $150K + $250K + $100K + $50K = $850K

Operating Profit = Gross Profit - Operating Expenses

Operating Profit = $4.75M - $850K = $3.9M

The operating profit is $3.9M.

EBIT and EBITDA

Operating profit is also called EBIT, which stands for Earnings Before Interest and Taxes. So, know that operating profit does not include interest payments or taxes.

Another financial term you should be familiar with is EBITDA. This stands for Earnings Before Interest, Taxes, Depreciation, and Amortization.

In other words, EBITDA is EBIT without depreciation and amortization subtracted from it.

Let's take a look at some examples calculating these things.

Example #1: Calculate this company's EBIT based on the information provided below.

- EBITDA: $2,500,000
- Depreciation: $300,000
- Amortization: $200,000

EBIT = EBITDA - Depreciation - Amortization

EBIT = $2,500,000 - $300,000 - $200,000 = $2,000,000

The company's EBIT is $2,000,000.

Let's take a look at another example.

Example #2: Calculate this company's EBIT and EBITDA based on the information provided below.

- Revenue: $10,000,000
- COGS: $4,000,000
- Operating expenses (excluding depreciation and amortization): $2,500,000
- Depreciation: $500,000
- Amortization: $200,000

- Interest expense: $300,000

- Taxes: $400,000

EBIT = Revenue − COGS − Operating Expenses (including depreciation and amortization)

EBIT = $10,000,000 − $4,000,000 − $2,500,000 − $500,000 − $200,000 = $2,800,000

EBITDA = EBIT + Depreciation + Amortization

EBITDA = $2,800,000 + $500,000 + $200,000 = $3,500,000

The company's EBIT is $2,800,000 and its EBITDA is $3,500,000.

Summary

- Gross profit is how much money a company makes after covering the direct costs of producing its product or service

- Gross Profit = Revenue – COGS

- Gross Margin = Gross Profit / Revenue

- Operating profit is the profit a company makes after covering both the direct and indirect costs of producing its product or service

- Operating Profit = Gross Profit – Operating Expenses

- Operating Margin = Operating Profit / Revenue

- Operating profit is also called EBIT, which stands for Earnings Before Interest and Taxes

- EBITDA stands for Earnings Before Interest, Taxes, Depreciation, and Amortization; it is EBIT without depreciation and amortization subtracted from it

Practice Problems

1. A company sells custom-made furniture. Last quarter, they reported the following:

   - Revenue: $800,000
   - Wood and materials: $300,000
   - Factory worker wages: $100,000
   - Sales and marketing: $70,000
   - Rent for headquarters: $50,000
   - Depreciation of machinery: $40,000
   - Office supplies: $10,000
   - Administrative salaries: $60,000
   - Interest on business loan: $20,000
   - Taxes: $30,000
   - Research and development costs: $40,000
   - Amortization of intellectual property: $10,000

   What is this company's gross profit?

2. In the previous problem, what is the company's operating profit?

3. In the previous problem, what is the company's EBITDA?

4. A tech startup has revenue of $5,000,000 and operating expenses of $2,000,000. If they have an operating margin of 20%, what is their COGS?

5. You are evaluating two acquisition targets in the same industry. Based on the following information, which company has the higher operating margin?

   Company A:

   - Revenue: $10M
   - COGS: $4M
   - Operating Expenses: $3M
   - Depreciation: $500K
   - Amortization: $100K

   Company B:

   - Revenue: $20M
   - COGS: $10M
   - Operating Expenses: $4M
   - Depreciation: $300K
   - Amortization: $100K

Solutions

1. **$400,000**

   COGS = $300,000 + $100,000 = $400,000

   Gross Profit = $800,000 - $400,000 = $400,000

2. **$120,000**

   Operating Expenses = $70,000 + $50,000 + $40,000 + $10,000 + $60,000 + $40,000 + $10,000 = $280,000

   Operating Profit = $400,000 - $280,000 = $120,000

3. **$170,000**

   EBITDA = EBIT + Depreciation + Amortization

   EBITA = $120,000 + $40,000 + $10,000 = $170,000

4. **$2,000,000**

   Operating Profit = $5,000,000 * 20% = $1,000,000

   Operating Profit = Revenue - COGS - Operating Expenses

   COGS = Revenue - Operating Expenses - Operating Profit

   COGS = $5,000,000 - $2,000,000 - $1,000,000 = $2,000,000

5. **Company B**

   Company A Operating Profit = $10M - $4M - $3M - $500K - $100K = $2.4M

   Company A Operating Margin = $2.4M / $10M = 24%

   Company B Operating Profit = $20M - $10M - $4M - $300K - $100K = $5.6M

Company B Operating Margin = $5.6M / $20M = 28%

Company B has a higher operating margin.

14. Charts and Graphs

Why Charts and Graphs Matter

Charts and graphs are a core part of consulting case interviews. Interviewers will often provide you with an exhibit or several exhibits for you to look at.

They might ask you:

- What's going on here?

- What insights can you draw?

- Where would you dig deeper?

Consultants rely heavily on visuals to communicate complex data clearly and efficiently. So, expect to do the same during a case interview.

You'll have to not just read a chart or graph, but interpret it, extract insights, and tie it back to the overall business problem. The good news is that you don't need to be a data scientist to succeed in this portion of the case interview.

You just need to be familiar with all of the different types of charts and graphs you might see. That is what the focus of this chapter is on.

Charts and Graphs You Should Know

Simple bar chart

A simple bar chart compares quantities across categories. The length of each bar represents a specific value, making it easy to compare different categories side by side.

What to look for:

- Which bars are the tallest or shortest?
- Are there large differences between the bars?

Example:

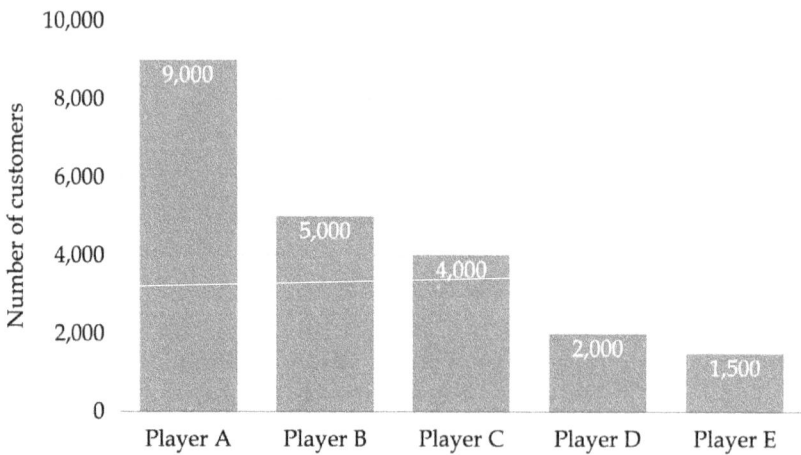

Key observations:

- Player A has the highest number of customers

- Player E has the lowest number of customers

- There are large differences between Player A and the other players

Stacked bar chart

A stacked bar chart compares quantities across categories while also breaking down each category into separate components. Each part of the bar represents a component and the total length of the bar shows the overall value.

What to look for:

- Which bars are the tallest or shortest?

- What components are the largest or smallest in each category?

- Are there large differences between the bars?

- Are there any changes in the proportions of each component across categories?

Example:

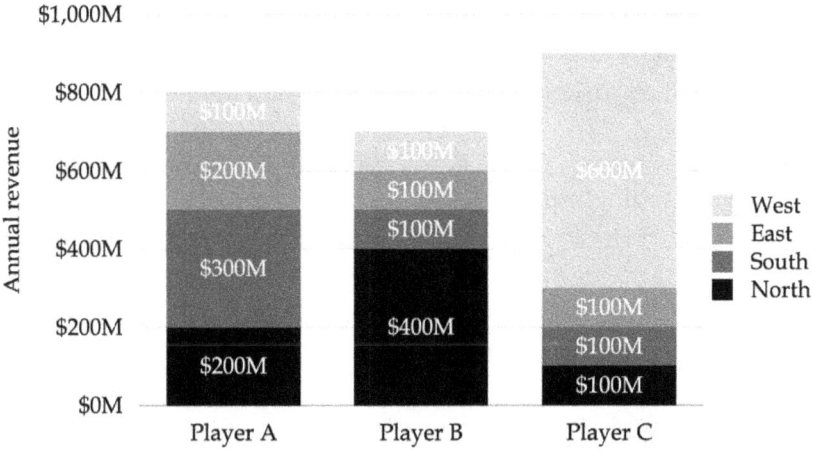

Key observations:

- Player C has the highest annual revenue
- Player B has the lowest annual revenue
- Total revenue across players is fairly similar
- Player B has the highest revenue in the North region
- Player A has the highest revenue in the South and East regions
- Player C has the highest revenue in the West region

100% stacked bar chart

A 100% stacked bar chart is similar to a stacked bar chart, but each bar is normalized to 100%.

This means that the total of each bar is the same, but the segments now show the relative proportion each component makes up of the entire bar.

What to look for:

- What components are the largest or smallest in each category?
- Are there large differences between the bars?
- Are there any changes in the proportions of each component across categories?

Example:

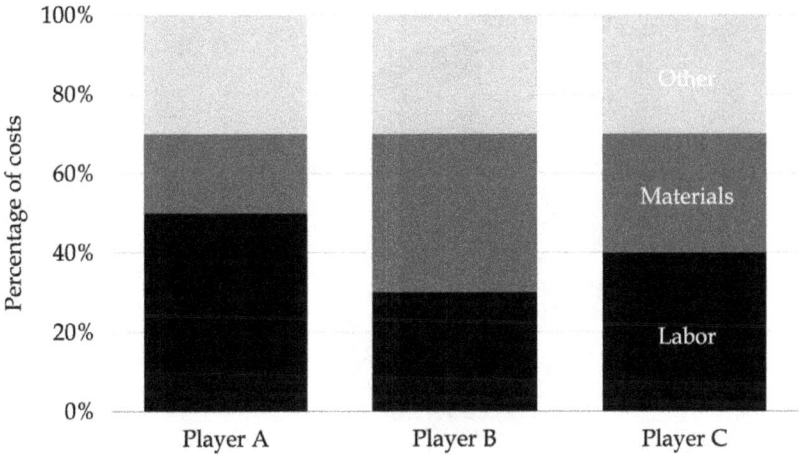

Key observations:

- Player A has the highest percentage of labor costs
- Player B has the highest percentage of materials costs
- All players have the same percentage of other costs

Pie chart

A pie chart is essentially a single stacked bar chart that is shown as pieces of a pie rather than segments in a bar.

In other words, a pie chart shows the relationship of parts to a whole. The whole is represented by the entire circle while each slice represents a part of the total.

What to look for:

- Which slices are the largest or smallest?
- How much variation in size is there among all of the slices?

Example:

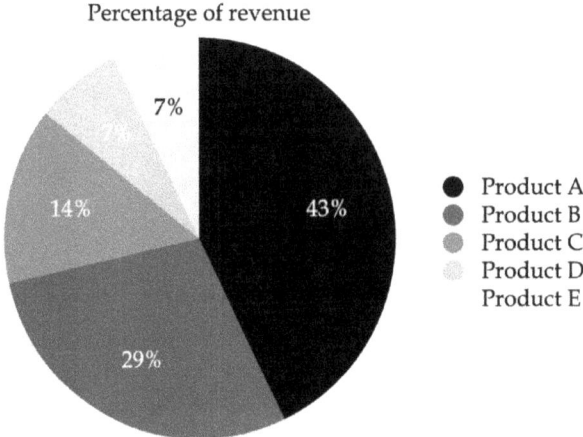

Key observations:

- Product A makes up the highest percentage of revenue

- Product D and Product E make up the lowest percentage of revenue

- Product A and B account for nearly 3/4 of total revenue

Marimekko / Mekko chart

A Marimekko or Mekko chart is a two-dimensional chart that shows both the size and proportion of different categories. The width of each column represents the size of the category and the height represents the proportion of each component.

You can think of a Marimekko or Mekko chart as a large pie chart. Instead of slices, you have rectangles that show two different numbers based on their width and length.

You can also think of a Marimekko or Mekko chart as a bar chart with another dimension of information. While bar charts only show different heights, Marimekko or Mekko charts show different heights and widths.

What to look for:

- How do the widths of each category compare?
- How do the heights of each component compare?
- How does the total area of each box compare?

Example:

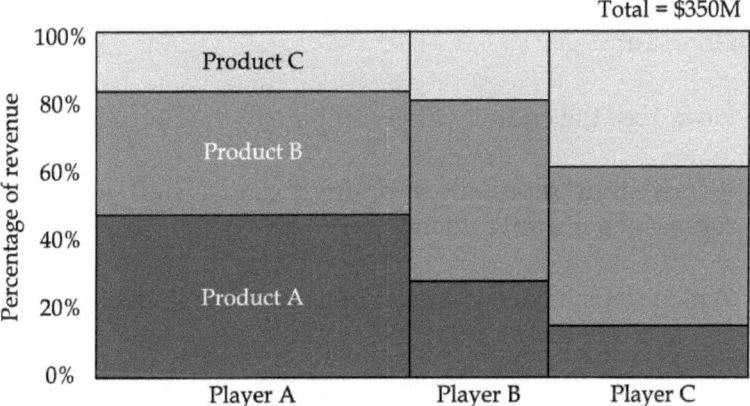

Key observations:

- Player A has the highest revenue
- Player B has the lowest revenue
- Player A has the highest percentage of revenue coming from Product A
- Player B has the highest percentage of revenue coming from Product B

- Player C has the highest percentage of revenue coming from Product C

- Player A's Product A generates the highest amount of revenue out of all products across all players

- Player B's Product C generates the lowest amount of revenue out of all products across all players

Waterfall chart

A waterfall chart shows how a starting value has increased or decreased by a series of positive or negative values. It is often used to show changes over time.

What to look for:

- How does the ending value compare to the starting value?

- Which steps represent a positive change and which steps represent a negative change?

- Which steps have the largest impact on the final outcome?

Example:

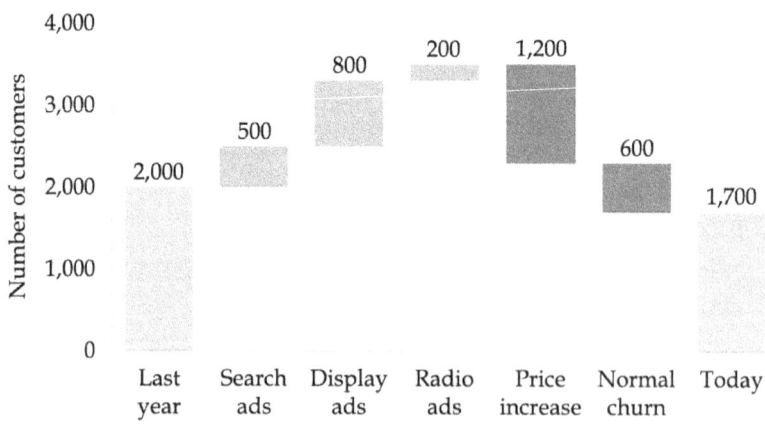

Key observations:

- The number of customers has decreased from 2,000 to 1,700

- All three types of ads contributed to an increase in the number of customers

- Price increases and normal churn contribute to a decrease in the number of customers

- Display ads are the largest driver contributing to an increase in the number of customers

- Price increases are the largest driver contributing to a decrease in the number of customers

Histogram

A histogram shows the distribution of data points across different ranges or intervals. It is used to see how often different ranges of data occur.

What to look for:

- What is the shape of the distribution?

- What ranges have the highest and lowest number of occurrences?

- Are there any outliers?

Example:

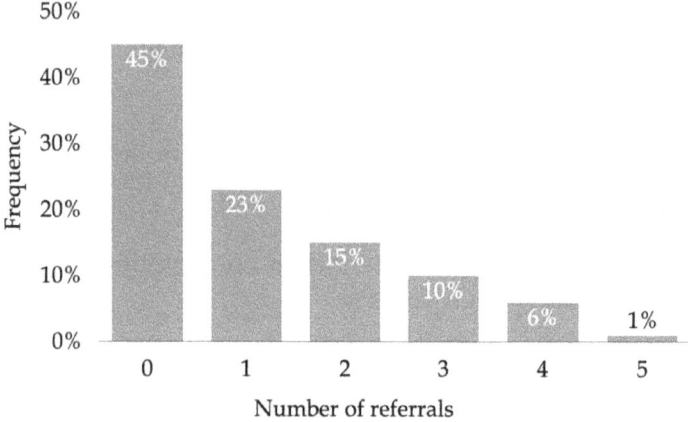

Key observations:

- As the number of referrals increases, frequency decreases significantly

- Having 0 referrals is the most common result, occurring 45% of the time

- Having 5 referrals is the least common result, occurring 1% of the time

Line graph

A line graph shows trends over time by plotting data points connected by lines.

What to look for:

- What is the overall trend?

- Are there any sharp peaks or dips?

- When does the line change direction?

Example:

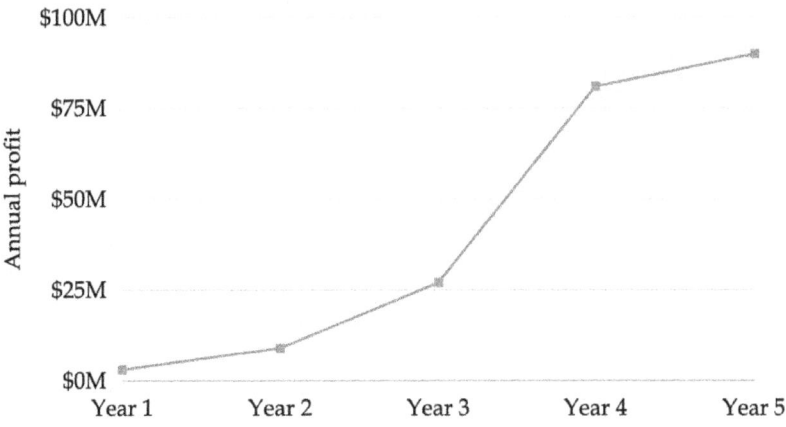

Key observations:

- Annual profit has increased every year
- Annual profit has increased almost exponentially from Year 1 to 4
- The rate of increase slowed down greatly in Year 5

Scatterplot

A scatterplot shows the relationship between two things. Each point represents a data point, with one quantity plotted on the x-axis and the other plotted on the y-axis.

What to look for:

- Are the data points clustered together or spread out?
- Are there any patterns that show a relationship between the two things being plotted?
- Are there any outliers?

Example:

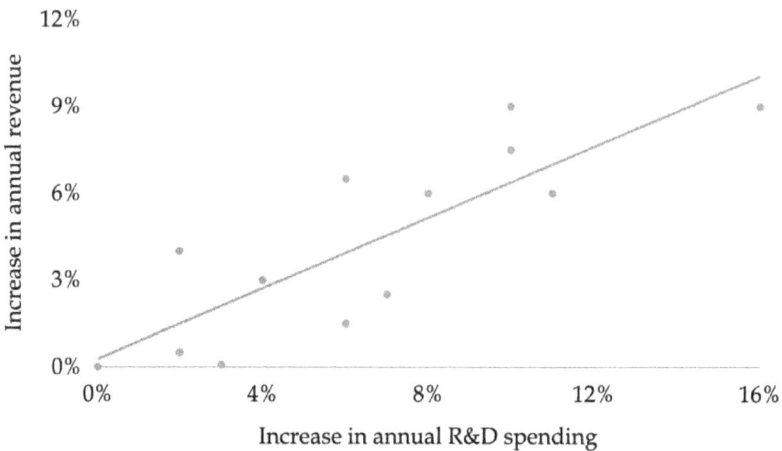

Key observations:

- As R&D spending increases, annual revenue increases

- All data points generally follow this trend and there is a fairly strong correlation

- There is one data point on the far right that is much further away from the rest of the data points

Bubble chart

A bubble chart is similar to a scatterplot but with additional dimensions of data added. Typically, the size of each bubble represents a third dimension of data.

For more complex bubble charts, the color of the bubble, outline of the bubble, or shading of the bubble can be used to show even more dimensions of data.

What to look for:

- Are the data points clustered together or spread out?

- Which bubbles are the largest or smallest?

- Are there any patterns that show a relationship between the different variables being shown?

- Are there any outliers?

Example:

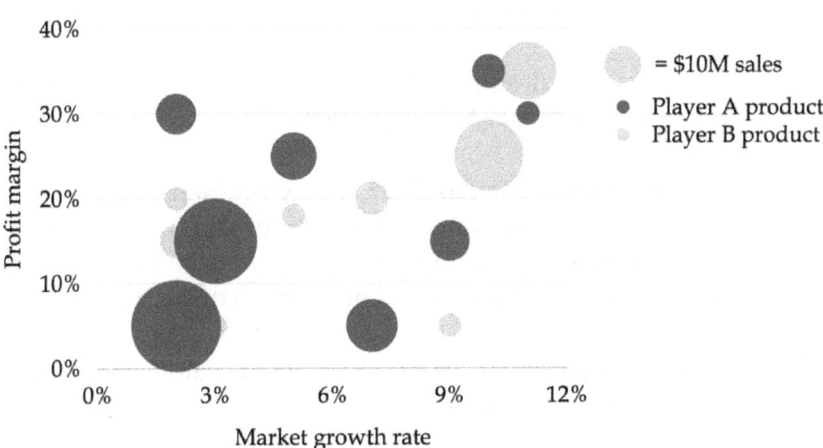

Key observations:

- Player A and Player B's products are spread out widely, having a wide range of profit margins and market growth rates

- Player A has more sales from products that have smaller profit margins and smaller market growth rates

- Player B has more sales from products that have larger profit margins and larger market growth rates

Summary

- A simple bar chart compares quantities across categories

- A stacked bar chart compares quantities across categories while also breaking down each category into separate components

- A 100% stacked bar chart is similar to a stacked bar chart, but each bar is normalized to 100%

- A pie chart is a single stacked bar chart that is shown as pieces of a pie rather than segments in a bar

- A Marimekko or Mekko chart is a two-dimensional chart that shows both the size and proportion of different categories - the width of each column represents the size of the category and the height represents the proportion of each component

- A waterfall chart shows how a starting value has increased or decreased by a series of positive or negative values

- A histogram shows the distribution of data points across different ranges or intervals

- A line graph shows trends over time by plotting data points connected by lines

- A scatterplot shows the relationship between two things, with one quantity plotted on the x-axis and the other plotted on the y-axis

- A bubble chart is similar to a scatterplot but with additional dimensions of data added

15. Market Sizing

Why Market Sizing Matters

Market sizing is the process of estimating how big a market is, usually in terms of annual revenue. It used to be a core component of case interviews, assessing your ability to work with numbers and communicate clearly.

Examples of market sizing questions include:

- What is the size of the sunglasses market?

- How much money is spent on laptops each year?

- What is the market size of wine?

Now a days, market sizing questions are not asked as often. However, you should still prepare for them because they do still show up from time to time.

In the real world, consultants are often asked to provide quick but informed estimates, whether it's estimating the market size for a new product, the potential revenue from a business idea, or the number of people who might use a service.

Market sizing questions might seem tough to answer at first, but with enough practice, these questions become straight forward and simple.

Interviewers aren't looking for a perfectly accurate answer. Instead, they want to see:

- Your problem-solving approach

- Your comfort with numbers

- Your communication skills

So, the process of how you get your answer is much more important than the answer that you come up with. You don't need to come close to the actual answer to do well in this type of case math.

This chapter will teach you the two main approaches to market sizing and how to use each method effectively in case interviews.

Top-Down Approach

A top-down approach is the most commonly used approach for market sizing and other estimation questions.

In a top-down approach, you begin with a large, known number and narrow it down using a series of logical filters and assumptions to estimate your target number.

In most cases, the large, known number that you start with is the U.S. or global population. You'll take this large figure and narrow it down until you get the desired population and then estimate their spending.

Let's take a look at an example to illustrate this approach:

What is the market size of non-electric toothbrushes in the United States?

In determining the market size of non-electric toothbrushes in the United States, a top-down market approach would look like the following:

- Start with the U.S. population

- Estimate what percentage of the population brushes their teeth

- Estimate what percentage of the population uses regular toothbrushes instead of electric toothbrushes

- Estimate how many toothbrushes the average person goes through in a year

- Estimate the cost per toothbrush

- Multiply all of these figures to determine the market size

A top-down approach is best when you have good general knowledge about the population or when it's difficult to estimate specifics.

Example #1: How many iPhones does Apple sell in the U.S. each year?

Using a top-down market sizing approach, you could come up with the following:

- Start with the number of people in the U.S.

- Estimate the percentage of people that have cell phones

- Estimate the percentage of cell phones that are iPhones

- Estimate the frequency in which a person purchases a new iPhone each year

- Multiply these numbers to determine the number of iPhones sold each year

Following this approach, we'll assume a U.S. population size of 320 million people.

If 80% of people have cell phones and 50% of cell phones are iPhones, this gives us 128 million iPhones.

If a person purchases a new iPhone every two years, that means 64 million iPhones are sold in the U.S. each year.

Let's take a look at another example.

Example #2: What is the volume of beer (in oz.) sold at an NBA basketball game?

A top-down estimation approach we can use to structure this problem is the following:

- Estimate the average number of seats at an NBA basketball game
- Estimate the average percentage of seats that are filled
- Estimate the percentage of people that are legally allowed to drink beer
- Estimate the percentage of people that would buy beer at an NBA basketball game
- Estimate the average number of beers purchased per person
- Estimate the volume of one beer
- Multiply all of these figures to determine the volume of beer sold at an NBA basketball game

Let's estimate that the average NBA basketball arena has 20,000 seats.

Assume that, on average, 70% of seats are filled. This means 70% * 20,000 = 14,000 people attend the average NBA basketball game.

Alcohol cannot be sold to people under the age of 21 in the U.S. If we assume that the average human life expectancy is 80 years and that there is a uniform distribution of ages, that means 20 / 80 = 25% of people cannot drink. Therefore, 75% of people can drink.

75% * 14,000 people = 10,500 people legally allowed to drink beer.

Let's estimate that perhaps 60% of these people would purchase a beer. That means 60% * 10,500 people = 6,300 people purchase beer.

If the average person purchases 1 beer, that means 6,300 beers are purchased.

One beer is approximately 12 oz. Therefore, 6,300 beers * 12 oz. = 75,600 oz. of beer is sold at an NBA basketball game.

Bottom-Up Approach

A bottom-up approach is not used as often in market sizing compared to a top-down approach. Still, it is helpful for specific situations.

In a bottom-up approach, you start with unit-level data and scale it up. In other words, you start by estimating usage or revenue based on the behavior of an individual user, household, or store and multiply to build up your answer.

Let's take a look at an example to illustrate this approach:

What is the market size of non-electric toothbrushes in the United States?

In determining the market size of non-electric toothbrushes in the United States, a bottom-up market sizing approach could look like the following:

- Start with a single individual

- Determine how many toothbrushes the average individual goes through in a year

- Estimate the cost per toothbrush

- Calculate the annual toothbrush spend of a single individual

- Estimate the number of individuals that purchase regular toothbrushes

- Multiply these figures to determine the market size of toothbrushes

A bottom-up approach is best when you can estimate user behavior or unit sales reliably or when the product or service is used regularly at a personal or store level.

Example #1: Estimate the annual market size for coffee sales at cafes in New York City.

A bottom-up estimation approach we can use to structure this problem is the following:

- Calculate the coffee revenue for a single cafe
    - Estimate how many cups of coffee are served per day
    - Estimate the average price per cup

- Estimate the number of cafes in New York City
    - Estimate the population of New York City
    - Estimate how many people 1 cafe can serve

- Multiply these figures to determine the market size for coffee sales in New York City

Let's assume that the average cafe serves 200 cups of coffee per day at a price of $4. Therefore, daily revenue is $800.

Multiplying this by 365 days to get annual revenue, we get $292,000. Let's round this to $300,000 for simplicity.

So, the average cafe generates $300,000 per year.

Let's assume the population of New York City is 8M. Let's assume that 1 cafe can serve 4,000 people. Therefore, there are 2,000 cafes in New York City.

Multiplying 2,000 cafes by $300,000 annual revenue per cafe, we get our final answer of $600M.

Let's take a look at another example.

Example #2: Estimate the annual market size for dog grooming services in the United States.

A bottom-up estimation approach we can use to structure this problem is the following:

- Calculate how much is spent on a single dog on grooming services

    o   Estimate the number of times a dog is groomed per year

    o   Estimate the cost per grooming

- Estimate the number of dogs in the U.S. that are taken to dog groomers

    o   Start with the U.S. population

    o   Estimate the number of households

    o   Estimate what percentage have dogs

- Estimate the average number of dogs per household
- Estimate what percentage pay for dog grooming
- Multiply these figures to determine the market size for dog grooming services in the United States

Let's assume that the average dog gets professionally groomed 4 times a year and that the average cost per grooming is $50.

That means that $200 is spent per dog each year on dog grooming services.

Assume the U.S. population is 320M and that the average household size is 2.5. That means there are 128M households.

Assume that 50% of households have dogs and that the average household has 1.2 dogs. Also, assume that 50% of those households pay for dog grooming services. Therefore, 38.4M dogs are professionally groomed.

Multiplying 38.4M dogs by $200 of spend per year gives us our final answer of $7.68B.

Summary

- Market sizing is the process of estimating how big a market is, usually in terms of annual revenue

- There are two approaches for market sizing:

    o In a top-down approach, begin with a large, known number and narrow it down using a series of logical filters and assumptions to estimate your target number

    o In a bottom-up approach, start with unit-level data and scale it up. In other words, you start by estimating usage or revenue based on the behavior of an individual user, household, or store and multiply to build up your answer

- A top-down approach is the most commonly used approach for market sizing and other estimation questions

Practice Problems

1. How many cans of soda are consumed in the U.S. each year?

2. What is the market size of disposable diapers in the U.S.?

3. How many car tires are sold in the U.S. each year?

4. How many TV ads are shown in the U.S. each day?

5. How many hot dogs does a hot dog stand located in a busy intersection in New York City sell in a year?

Solutions

1. **~58.24B cans (no single correct answer)**

   One potential approach could look like the following:

   - Start with the U.S. population
   - Estimate the percentage of people that drink soda
   - Estimate the number of cans a person drinks per day
   - Multiply by 7 to get the number of cans per week
   - Multiply by 52 to get the number of cans per year

   Let's assume the U.S. population is 320M and that half of the population drinks soda. That gives us 160M people that drink soda.

   Assume that the average person drinks 1 can per day, which is 7 cans per week.

   160M people * 7 cans per week = 1.12B cans per week.

   Next, we can multiply by 52 weeks per year to get the number of cans per year.

   1.12B cans per week * 52 weeks per year = 58.24B cans per year.

2. **~$3B (no single correct answer)**

   One potential approach could look like the following:

   - Start with the U.S. population
   - Segment the population by age

- Estimate the number of people that wear disposable diapers

- Estimate the number of disposable diapers used per day

- Multiply by 7 to get the number of diapers used per week

- Multiply by 52 to get the number of diapers used per year

- Multiply by the average price per disposable diaper

Let's start by assuming the U.S. population is 320M. Let's also assume the average life expectancy is 80 years and that there is an even distribution of ages.

This means that there are 4M people at each age.

Diapers are primarily worn by babies. There is a small percentage of adults that might wear disposable diapers, but let's assume that number is negligible compared to the number of babies.

Babies typically stop wearing diapers after age 2. So, the population of babies under 2 years is 2 * 4M = 8M.

Let's assume babies go through 2 diapers per day. Multiplying this by 7, that is 14 diapers per week. Multiplying this by 52, that is 728 diapers per year.

8M babies * 728 diapers per year = 5.824B diapers per year. Let's round this to 6B diapers to make our calculations a bit easier.

Let's assume the average disposable diaper costs $0.50.

6B * $0.50 = $3B

3. **~120M tires (no single correct answer)**

   One potential approach could look like the following:

   - Start with the U.S. population
   - Estimate the number of households
   - Estimate the percentage of households that own a car
   - Estimate the average number of cars per household
   - Multiply by 4 to get the number of tires per household
   - Estimate the frequency that tires are replaced

   Let's start with a U.S. population of 320M. Assume that the average household size is 2.5 people. That means there are 320M / 2.5 = 128M households.

   Let's assume that 80% of households have a car. That gives us 128M * 80% = 102.4M households that have a car. Let's round this to 100M households to make our calculations simpler.

   Let's assume the average household has 1.5 cars. This gives us 100M * 1.5 = 150M cars.

   Multiplying this by 4 gives us 600M tires.

   Assume that tires are replaced every 5 years.

   So, 600M / 5 = 120M tires are purchased each year.

4. **~1.44M (no single correct answer)**

   One potential approach could look like the following:

   - Estimate the number of TV channels in the U.S.

- Assume each channel is on-air for 24 hours each day
- Estimate the percentage of airtime that is given to ads
- Estimate the average duration of an ad
- Divide total ad airtime by ad duration to determine how many TV ads are shown

Starting with the number of TV channels in the U.S., let's assume there are roughly 2,000 TV channels in the U.S. This estimate could be based on the number of channels that you get from your cable TV services.

Assuming each channel is on-air for 24 hours each day, that gives us 2,000 * 24 = 48,000 hours of airtime each day.

Based on personal experience, ads take up approximately 25% of total airtime. Therefore, ads run for 48,000 hours * 25% = 12,000 hours each day.

The average duration of an ad can be estimated to be approximately 30 seconds. Therefore, we need to divide 12,000 hours by 30 seconds to get the total number of ads run in a day.

12,000 hours is the equivalent of 60 * 12,000 = 720,000 minutes. 30 seconds is equivalent to 0.5 minutes.

So, 720,000 minutes divided by 0.5 minutes gives us 1.44M TV ads that are shown in the U.S. each day.

5. **~42,000 hot dogs (no single correct answer)**

   One potential approach could look like the following:

   - Start with the number of hours a stand is open in a day

- Estimate the number of hours that is busy vs. not busy

- Estimate the number of hot dogs sold per hour

- Multiply by 7 to get the number of hot dogs sold per week

- Estimate the number of weeks the hot dog stand is open for

- Multiply by the number of weeks to get the number per year

Let's assume that a hot dog stand is open for 12 hours every day. Let's assume that 4 of these hours are busy hours while the other 8 are non-busy hours.

During busy hours, assume that the hot dog stand sells 20 hot dogs per hour. During non-busy hours, assume that the hot dog stand sells 5 hot dogs per hour.

So, (4 * 20) + (8 * 5) = 120 hot dogs per day.

Multiplying by 7, this gives us 840 hot dogs per week.

Let's assume the hot dog stand is open for 50 weeks a year. It is closed for holidays and vacations for the other weeks.

840 hot dogs per week * 50 weeks = 42,000 hot dogs per year.

16. Mental Math Strategies

Why Mental Math Matters

In consulting case interviews, speed and accuracy matter.

You need to correctly perform your math calculations to demonstrate that you're competent and comfortable working with numbers. However, you also can't be taking forever when doing simple calculations.

This is where mental math comes in.

For simple calculations, using mental math can save you a lot of time. This will enable you to spend more of your time solving the math problem rather than crunching numbers.

You don't need to always be doing mental math. Remember, you have paper and a pen to use for any calculations. However, if you can use mental math to save time while also maintaining your accuracy, you'll have an advantage over the competition.

In this chapter, we'll cover the very best strategies you can use to get better at mental math. These are practical shortcuts that are guaranteed to save you some time:

- Do math with letters

- Use the distributive property

- Use round numbers for calculations

- Break up division into multiple steps

- Flip percentages

- Know the 10%, 5%, and 1% rule

- Memorize common fractions

- Use the Rule of 72

Do Math with Letters

Having too many zeros or two few zeros in your math calculations is by far the most common math mistake in a case interview. This one math mistake could make the difference between receiving a consulting job offer and getting rejected.

To avoid making this mistake, do math with letters. What do we mean by this?

You can simplify how you write large numbers by using letters to represent thousands, millions, billions, and trillions. For example:

- 10,000 can be expressed as 10K

- 200,000,000 can be expressed as 200M

- 30,000,000,000 can be expressed as 30B

- 4,000,000,000,000 can be expressed as 4T

Once you've written the large numbers you are working with by these letters, there are only a few multiplication shortcuts you need to remember:

- K * K = M
- M * K = B
- B * K = T
- M * M = T

Additionally, there are only a few division shortcuts you need to remember:

- M / K = K
- B / K = M
- B / M = K
- T / K = B
- T / M = M
- T / B = K

Here are a few examples to illustrate how doing math with letters will simplify your calculations with large numbers and greatly reduce the number of errors you make.

Example #1: A car dealership sold 12,000 cars last year at a price of $18,000 each. How much revenue have they generated?

Revenue = 12,000 * 18,000

Revenue = 12K * 18K

Revenue = (12 * 18) * (K * K)

Revenue = 216 * M

Revenue = 216M

Let's take a look at another example.

Example #2: A company has $1,680,000,000 in sales across 120,000 customer accounts. What is the average spend per customer account?

Average Spend = $1,680,000,000 / 120,000

Average Spend = $1,680M / 120K

Average Spend = ($1,680/120) * (M / K)

Average Spend = $14 * K

Average Spend = $14K

Use the Distributive Property

It's helpful to be able to multiply numbers quickly during a case interview. To increase your speed, you may find it helpful to use the distributive property when multiplying numbers.

The distributive property states:

A * (B + C) = (A * B) + (A * C)

This can help break up complex multiplication into simpler and more manageable steps.

Example #1: 11 * 23

23 * (1 + 10)

(23 * 1) + (10 * 23)

23 + 230

253

Let's take a look at another example.

Example #2: 15 * 304

15 * (300 + 4)

(15 * 300) + (15 * 4)

4,500 + 60

4,560

Use Round Numbers for Calculations

When adding or multiplying numbers where one of the numbers is close to a nice round number, it may be easier to round that number up or down.

After you calculate the sum or product using the rounded number, you can make adjustments to the answer to account for the rounding that you did.

This approach involves more steps, but each step in the calculation is simpler and less prone to making errors.

Example #1: 499 + 398

Let's round 499 to 500 and 398 to 400.

500 + 400 = 900

Since the rounding that we did increased our answer by 3, we need to subtract 3 to get the actual answer.

900 − 3

897

Let's take a look at another example.

Example #2: 49 * 7

Let's round 49 to 50.

50 * 7

350

Since we rounded 49 to 50, we increased our answer by 7 since we are multiplying the number that we rounded by 7. So, we need to subtract 7 from our answer to get the final answer.

350 − 7

343

Break Up Division into Multiple Steps

When dividing two numbers, try to simplify the division by dividing both numbers by a smaller number to make them smaller. This can be repeated to make the numbers even smaller.

Eventually, you'll either complete the division or be left with a smaller division problem to calculate.

Example #1: 448 / 56

224 / 28

112 / 14

56 / 7

8

Let's take a look at another example.

Example #2: 432 / 12

216 / 6

108 / 3

36

Flip Percentages

When multiplying a percentage by a number, you can flip the numbers. For example, instead of finding X% of Y, this is the same as finding Y% of X.

In a case interview, you might find certain situations where it is easier to multiply two numbers if you flip the percentages.

Example #1: 16% * 25

25% * 16

4

Let's take a look at another example.

Example #2: 120% * 50

50% * 120

60

Know the 10%, 5%, and 1% Rules

You should know how to find 10%, 5%, and 1% of a number very quickly. These percentages are used a lot in case interviews.

- **10% Rule**: To easily find 10% of any number, move the decimal point one place to the left

- **5% Rule**: To easily find 5% of any number, find 10% of that number and then divide by 2

- **1% Rule**: To easily find 1% of any number, move the decimal point two places to the left

Example #1: What is 5% of 362?

10% of 362 is 36.2

Half of 36.2 is 18.1.

Let's take a look at another example.

Example #2: What is 3% of 1,040?

1% of 1,040 is 10.4.

To find 3%, we just need to multiply it by 3.

10.4 * 3 = 31.2

Memorize Common Fractions

To save yourself time in a case interview, you should memorize the decimal equivalents of common fractions.

If any of these fractions ever show up in a case interview, you won't need to manually calculate their decimal equivalents if you have to convert the fractions to a decimal or percentage.

The common fractions you should know are:

- 1/10 = 0.1
- 1/8 = 0.125
- 1/5 = 0.2
- 1/4 = 0.25
- 1/3 = 0.333 (repeating)
- 3/8 = 0.375
- 2/5 = 0.4
- 1/2 = 0.5
- 3/5 = 0.6
- 5/8 = 0.625
- 2/3 = 0.666 (repeating)
- 3/4 = 0.75
- 7/8 = 0.875
- 4/5 = 0.8

Use the Rule of 72

The Rule of 72 is a simple formula used to estimate the number of years required for something to double when given a growth rate.

All you need to do is to divide 72 by the annual growth rate to find the approximate time that it would take for something to double.

Example #1: An investment is expected to grow at 6% per year. How many years will it take to double in value?

Time to Double = 72 / 6

Time to Double = 12

The investment will take roughly 12 years to double in value.

Let's take a look at another example.

Example #2: A company with $100M in revenue is growing at 12% per year. At this rate, how long would it take for the company to reach $400M in revenue.

Time to Double = 72 / 12

Time to Double = 6

The company will need to double twice to reach $400M.

It will take the company roughly 6 * 2 = 12 years to reach $400M in revenue.

Summary

- Using mental math can save you a lot of time, enabling you to spend more of your time solving the math problem rather than crunching numbers

- Use the following mental math strategies and shortcuts when applicable:

    o   Do math with letters

    o   Use the distributive property

    o   Use round numbers for calculations

    o   Break up division into multiple steps

    o   Flip percentages

    o   Know the 10%, 5%, and 1% rule

    o   Memorize common fractions

    o   Use the Rule of 72

Practice Problems

1. 14,000 * 5,000,000,000

2. 42,000,000,000 / 70,000

3. 150,000 * 4,000,000

4. 480,000,000,000 / 1,600,000

5. 14 * 25

6. 107 * 400

7. 11 * 7,700

8. 398 + 4,997

9. 199 + 15,998

10. 5,997 + 399

11. 672 / 42

12. 1,728 / 144

13. 600 / 24

14. 36% * 50

15. 112% * 25

16. 15% * 4,080

17. 11% * 24

18. 1/8 * 1,000

19. If a company grows at 4% per year, estimate how long it will take to quadruple revenue.

20. How long will it take a company to go from $1M to $32M in revenue if it grows at 9% per year?

Solutions

1. **70T**

   14K * 5B

   (14 * 5) * (K * B)

   70T

2. **600K**

   (42B / 7K) / 10

   6M / 10

   600K

3. **600B**

   150K * 4M

   (150 * 4) * (K * M)

   600B

4. **300K**

   (480B / 16M) * 10

   30K * 10

   300K

5. **350**

   (10 * 25) + (4 * 25)

   250 + 100

350

6. **42,800**

   (100 * 400) + (7 * 400)

   40,000 + 2,800

   42,800

7. **84,700**

   (10 * 7,700) + (1 * 7,700)

   77,000 + 7,700

   84,700

8. **5,395**

   (400 + 5,000) − (2 + 3)

   5,400 − 5

   5,395

9. **16,197**

   (200 + 16,000) − (1 + 2)

   16,200 − 3

   16,197

10. **6,396**

    (6,000 + 400) − (3 + 1)

    6,400 − 4

6,396

11. **16**

　336 / 21

　112 / 7

　16

12. **12**

　864 / 72

　432 / 36

　216 / 18

　108 / 9

　36 / 3

　12

13. **25**

　300 / 12

　150 / 6

　50 / 2

　25

14. **18**

　50% * 36

　18

15. **28**

    25% * 112

    28

16. **612**

    (10% * 4,080) + (5% * 4,080)

    408 + 204

    612

17. **2.64**

    (10% * 24) + (1% * 24)

    2.4 + 0.24

    2.64

18. **125**

    0.125 * 1,000

    125

19. **~36 years**

    72 / 4 = 18 years to double

    18 * 2 = 36 years to quadruple

20. **40 years**

    72 / 9 = 8 years to double

    5 doublings needed to grow by 32x

5 * 8 = 40 years

17. Case Math Strategies

Why Being Strategic with Math Matters

Even if you have mastered all of the math concepts and formulas that show up in case interviews, there are a few math strategies that you can use to set yourself up for success.

These strategies can make case interview math easier for you, reduce your likelihood of making errors or mistakes, and help you impress your interviewers.

In this chapter, we'll cover five strategies you should be using whenever you do any case math:

- Develop a structure before doing any math

- Talk through your calculations out loud

- Round numbers when appropriate

- Sense check your numbers along the way

- Talk through the implications of your answer

Let's talk through each of these strategies in more detail.

Develop a Structure Before Doing Any Math

Do not begin doing any math calculations until you have developed an approach or structure. This will prevent you from making unnecessary calculations and help you avoid making math mistakes.

When you're given numbers in a case interview, you may get excited and want to start adding and multiplying things right away.

Avoid this temptation.

Instead, take the time to think through what you are being asked to calculate and figure out how you are going to get the final answer.

It looks really bad if you start doing calculations, get stuck, back track, do some more calculations, get stuck, and then spend a few minutes in silence trying to figure out what to do next.

Instead, if you ask the interviewer for a moment to collect your thoughts, you can write out the entire equation or series of steps that you'll take to reach the final answer.

Then, you can walk the interviewer through your approach and get their feedback on whether it makes sense to them. Once the interviewer has agreed that your approach makes sense, the rest of the problem is simple arithmetic.

If your approach is slightly wrong, the interviewer may give you some suggestions or hints to point you in the right direction. They aren't able to do this if you don't explain your thought process out loud.

Talk Through Your Calculations Out Loud

Case interviews are live performances. You are not solving problems silently, but thinking and discussing them out loud with the interviewer.

This means that you should talk through all math calculations out loud. This provides three benefits.

One, it decreases the likelihood that you'll make a mistake. Talking through what you are doing out loud helps you catch mistakes or errors that you would not have noticed if you had done the math in silence.

Two, it makes it easier for the interviewer to follow what you are doing. If you happen to get stuck or make a mistake, the interviewer can jump in to offer suggestions or guidance.

The interviewer cannot do this if you are not communicating exactly what you are doing.

Three, talking through your calculations out loud gives you credit for the work that you are doing. You may have some really great thoughts and ideas in your head, but you won't get any credit for them if you're just thinking about them in silence.

By talking through your thoughts and ideas as you are doing the math, the interviewer can see exactly what you are thinking.

Round Numbers When Appropriate

If possible, use round numbers to keep the math easy and reduce the likelihood that you make a calculation error.

For example, if you are making assumptions about the size of the United States population, use 320 million instead of 319 million.

If you are multiplying 199 by 17, ask if the interviewer will allow you to round so that you are multiplying 200 by 17.

Case interview math is already stressful, so why make the math more difficult for yourself if you don't have to?

You don't want to round too much since this may signal to the interviewer that you are uncomfortable performing math calculations if the numbers are not easy and round.

However, rounding occasionally can help simplify the calculations and reduce the likelihood that you make a calculation error.

Sense Check Your Numbers Along the Way

Accidentally missing zeroes or adding extra zeroes during your calculations is the most common math mistake. These mistakes will make your answer wildly off from the correct answer.

To avoid this, try to do a quick sense check after each step of a math calculation to see if your answer is in the right order of magnitude.

For example, if you are multiplying 125,000,000 by 24, you should expect your answer to be in the billions because 100 million * 20 = 2 billion.

If you are dividing $1 million by 18,000, you should expect your answer to be in the tens because $1,000K / 20K = 50.

If you do happen to initially make a math mistake, but end up catching the error when you sense check it, this will impress your interviewer.

They'll see that you're thoughtful, methodical, and capable of checking and correcting your own work. These are all traits that are highly valued in consulting.

Talk Through the Implications of Your Answer

When the interviewer gives you a quantitative problem during a case interview, don't just calculate the answer and stop there. After calculating the answer, ask yourself: "so what?"

How does your answer help you solve the overall case? What implications does your answer have for your potential recommendation?

You should always be tying the answer back to the objective of the case.

For example, if you are asked to calculate the market size of a new market that your client is considering entering, don't just give the answer and stop there.

Based on the market size that you calculated, is the market small or large? Is it an attractive market to enter? Should the client enter the market?

These are all implications that you should immediately talk about after calculating your answer.

Remember that each question asked in a case interview should get you closer to the final recommendation that you give at the end of the case. So, take what you've calculated and talk through how that impacts the final recommendation.

Summary

- Develop a structure before doing any math
- Talk through your calculations out loud
- Round numbers when appropriate
- Sense check your numbers along the way
- Talk through the implications of your answer

18. Practice Problems

Introduction to Practice Problems

In this chapter, we've provided you with 50 practice problems to practice all of the math fundamentals, formulas, and strategies that we've covered in this book.

These are realistic math problems that are based on actual case interview questions given by top-tier consulting firms such as McKinsey, BCG, and Bain.

I've roughly ordered these problems from easy to hard. So, you'll find that the problems get a bit more challenging as you work through them.

To get the most out of these practice problems, I highly recommend treating these practice problems like a live case interview.

Put away all of your notes, refrain from using a calculator, practice asking for time to structure your thoughts, and talk through the calculations out loud as you are doing them.

You should not be doing these practice problems in silence. Treat this practice like a live interview, not a math exam.

Once you've completely finished a practice problem, you'll find the solutions immediately after it.

Even if you got the right answer, take the time to compare how your approach differs from the model answer. See if there were any shortcuts you missed or opportunities to solve the math problem more quickly or efficiently.

You got this!

Practice Problem #1

An electric utility company has received a permit to build its first nuclear power plant. The cost of the plant is estimated to be about $7 billion. However, the company's management believes that there are cost overrun risks involved:

Construction type	Quoted cost	Risk of cost overrun	Cost of overrun
Technology & engineering	$4 billion	50%	$800 million
Structure	$2 billion	50%	$600 million
Other overhead	$1 billion	20%	$250 million
Total	$7 billion		

What is the expected value of the cost of the plant?

Solution to #1

Expected value = $7B + (50% * $800M) + (50% * $600M) + (20% * $250M)

Expected value = $7B + $400M + $300M + $50M

Expected value = $7.75B

$7.75B

Practice Problem #2

An oil and gas services provider is seeing a very high attrition rate among their engineers. See the chart below:

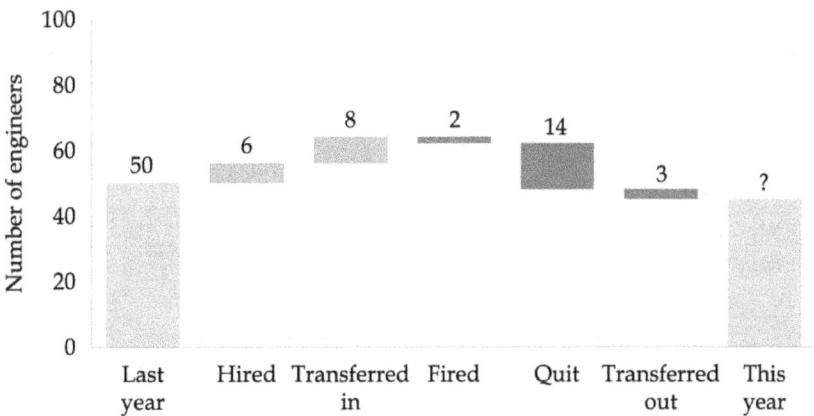

Part A: How many engineers do they have this year?

Part B: What is the attrition rate? Attrition rate is defined as the percentage of engineers that quit or transfer out.

Solution to #2

Part A

Engineers = 50 + 6 + 8 − 2 − 14 − 3 = 45

There are 45 engineers this year.

Part B

Attrition = (14 + 3) / 50 = 34%

The attrition rate is 34%.

Practice Problem #3

Our client is a large manufacturer of heavy-duty trucks that is concerned with their costs. Their total cost per truck is $40,000.

Based on the exhibits below, what is the potential savings for our client if they were to be best in industry in their parts cost?

Manufacturing mix	Client	Competitor A	Competitor B
In-house parts	70%	50%	30%
Outsourced parts	30%	50%	70%

Parts Cost Index	Client	Competitor A	Competitor B
In-house	100	100	80
Outsourced	120	80	100

Solution to #3

Let's calculate the client's costs for in-house parts and outsourced parts.

- In-house parts costs = $40,000 * 70% = $28,000

- Outsourced parts costs = $40,00 * 30% = $12,000

Let's calculate the costs for in-house parts and outsourced parts if we use the lowest costs from competitors.

- Cost savings for in-house: $28,000 * (80 / 100) = $22,400

- Cost savings for outsourced: $12,000 * (80 / 120) = $8,000

Finally, we can calculate the total cost savings.

Cost savings = $40,000 - $22,400 - $8,000 = $9,600

$9,600

Practice Problem #4

A hospital group generates $425M per year by providing patient care. Physicians at the hospital group spend 75% of their time on patient care, 15% on billing, and 10% on administrative tasks.

The hospital group is considering spending $50M per year to outsource billing so that physicians can see more patients. Assume that physicians do not take on additional costs from seeing more patients.

With the extra time, assume that physicians would spend that time proportionally across patient care and administrative tasks.

What is the potential ROI of outsourcing billing?

Solution to #4

Let's calculate how physicians spend their time if billing is completely outsourced.

% of time on patient care = 75% / 85% = 15/17

% of time on administrative tasks = 10% / 85% = 2/17

Next, let's set up a proportion to see how much revenue is generated if % of time on patient care increases from 75% to 15/17.

$425M / 75\% = x / (15/17)$

$x = \$500M$

Finally, we can calculate the ROI.

ROI = ($75M - $50M) / $50M = 50%

The ROI is 50%.

Practice Problem #5

Determine the number of gallons of ethanol in gasoline that were consumed in the U.S. last year. Last year, the number of miles driven in the U.S. was 1.8 trillion miles at an average of 20 miles per gallon.

There are two ethanol-gasoline blends:

- E-85 is 85% ethanol and accounts for 10% of the market

- E-15 is 15% ethanol and accounts for 90% of the market

Solution to #5

Let's first calculate the gallons of gasoline consumed last year.

Gallons of gasoline = 1.8 trillion miles / 20 miles per gallon = 90 billion gallons

Then, we can calculate the amount of ethanol consumed in each type of ethanol-gasoline blend:

- E-85: 90 billion gallons * 10% * 85% ethanol = 7.65B gallons

- E-15: 90 billion gallons * 90% * 15% ethanol = 12.15B gallons

Adding these two up, we get our answer.

Gallons of ethanol = 7.65B + 12.15B = 19.8B gallons

19.8B gallons of ethanol

Practice Problem #6

Our client is a private equity firm that is considering purchasing the Golden State Warriors, an NBA team. They believe that they can boost revenues while cutting costs.

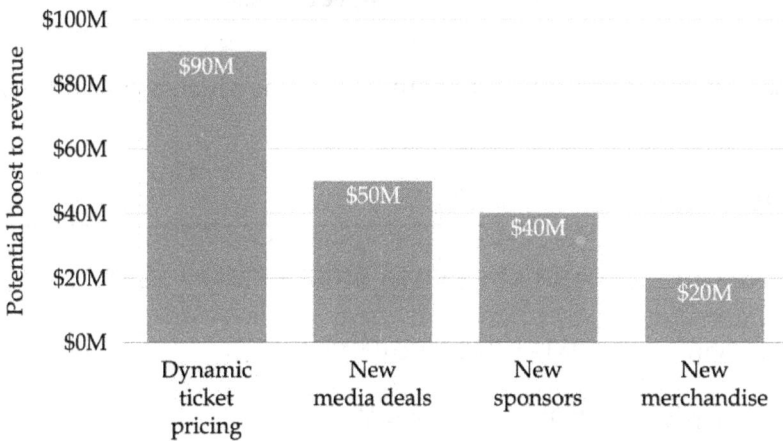

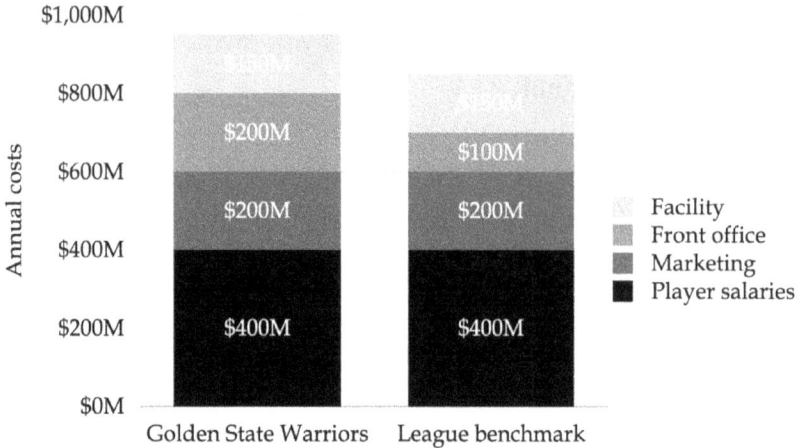

Based on the charts below, how much can they increase profits by?

Solution to #6

Revenue increase = $90M + $50M + $40M + $20M = $200M

Cost savings = $200M - $100M = $100M

Profit increase = $200M + $100M = $300M

$300M increase in profits

Practice Problem #7

Our client is a global luxury cruise line. They buy ships and offer tours around the world to individuals on vacation. Here is some information on the company:

- Revenue: $8B

- COGS: None

- Operating Costs: $7.25B
- Invested Capital: $15B

Part A: What is our client's return on invested capital (ROIC)? ROIC can be calculated by taking operating profit and dividing by the invested capital.

Part B: By what percentage do costs need to be reduced by to reach a 10% ROIC? Round to the nearest percent.

Part C: By what percentage do revenues need to increase by to reach a 10% ROIC? Round to the nearest percent.

Solution to #7

Part A

ROIC = Operating Profit / Invested Capital

ROIC = ($8B - $7.25B) / $15B = 5%

The ROIC is 5%.

Part B

Let's first calculate what costs need to be in order to achieve a 10% ROIC.

($8B − x) / $15B = 10%

x = $6.5B

Next, we can calculate the percent change in costs.

Percent change = ($6.5B - $7.25B) / $7.25B = -10% (rounded)

Costs need to decrease by 10%.

Part C

Let's calculate what revenue needs to be in order to achieve a 10% ROIC.

(x - $7.25B) / $15B = 10%

x = $8.75B

Next, we can calculate the percent change in revenue.

Percent change = ($8.75B - $8B) / $8B = 9% (rounded)

Revenue needs to increase by 9%.

Practice Problem #8

Our client is considering starting a new train company that travels between Philadelphia and Boston. Here is some information on the business:

- The initial investment per train is $50M
- Marketing costs $20M per year
- Operations and maintenance cost $10M per train per year
- Our client plans to have 3 trains
- Trains make 4 trips per day
- Trains run for 360 days per year
- Trains have a capacity of 500 people
- Our client is considering one of three ticket prices:
    - If tickets cost $40, there will be a 95% occupancy

- If tickets cost $50, there will be an 80% occupancy
- If tickets cost $60, there will be a 60% occupancy

With the optimal ticket price that maximizes profit, what is the payback period to recoup their initial investment?

Solution to #8

Let's first determine the optimal ticket price.

- $40 tickets: $40 * (500 * .95) = $19,000 per trip
- $50 tickets: $50 * (500 * 0.8) = $20,000 per trip
- $60 tickets: $60 * (500 * 0.6) = $18,000 per trip

To maximize profit, tickets should be priced at $50.

Revenue = 360 days * 3 trains * 4 trips per day * $20,000 per trip = $86.4M

Costs = $20M + (3 * $10M) = $50M

Profit = $86.4M - $50M = $36.4M

Payback period = (3 * $50M) / $36.4M = 4.1 (rounded)

The payback period is about 4.1 years.

Practice Problem #9

Our client is a mining company whose main product is copper ore. Based on the chart below, what is their current market share?

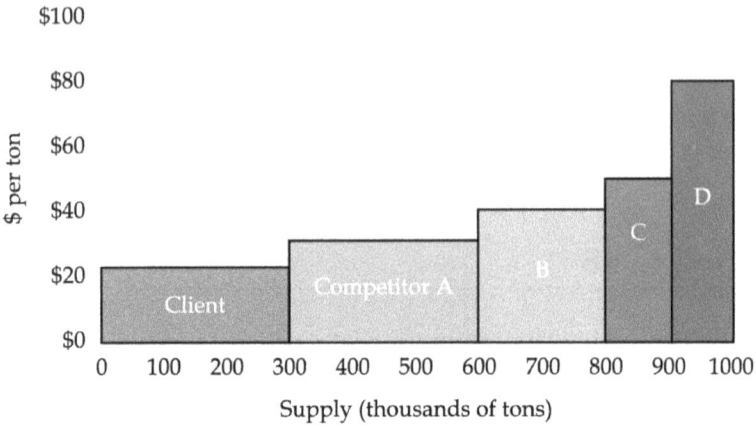

Solution to #9

Client revenue = $20 * 300K = $6M

Competitor A revenue = $30 * 300K = $9M

Competitor B revenue = $40 * 200K = $8M

Competitor C revenue = $50 * 100K = $5M

Competitor D revenue = $80 * 100K = $8M

Client market share = $6M / ($6M + $9M + $8M + $5M + $8M) = 1/6 = 16.7% (rounded)

They have about a 16.7% market share.

Practice Problem #10

Our client is a small art museum in Washington D.C. that specializes in European art. They generate all of their revenue through their membership fee of $150 per year. The cost to cover a membership is

$37.50 per year. Any profit is put into a fund to go towards future expenses.

Historically, our client has put in $150,000 into that fund every year. However, last year they were only able to put away 50% of what they normally put into the fund.

Our client is considering lowering membership fees by 20%. What is the percent increase in membership needed to bring the fund's annual deposit back to original levels?

Solution to #10

Current membership = ($150,000 * 50%) / ($150 - $37.50) = 667 (rounded)

Future membership = $150,000 / [($150 * 0.8) - $37.50] = 1,818 (rounded)

Percent change = (1,818 - 667) / 667 = 173% (rounded)

Membership would need to increase by 173%.

Practice Problem #11

Our client is a large global healthcare delivery non-profit that works on reducing the incidence of disease in developing nations. This year, they are focusing on spending $100M to reduce the incidence of malaria in Africa. About 40% of people in Africa get malaria each year.

Part A: Our client is considering investing in bed nets, which cost $5 each and last for 2 years. Bed nets are 40% effective at preventing the spread of malaria if used correctly. However, only 50% of people that use these bed nets use them correctly. Assume that there is an average of 1.5 people per bed.

How many cases of malaria would these bed nets avert?

Part B: A vaccine is 80% effective at preventing malaria. Assume the vaccine will always be administered correctly since clinicians will be present during vaccination. The vaccine costs $20 per dose and provides protection for 4 years.

How many cases of malaria would this vaccine avert?

Solution to #11

Part A

$100M / $5 = 20M bed nets

20M bed nets * 1.5 people per bed * 40% incidence rate * 40% effectiveness * 50% proper usage * 2 years per bed = 4.8M cases

4.8M cases

Part B

$100M / $20 = 5M doses

5M doses * 40% incidence rate * 80% effectiveness * 4 years per vaccine = 6.4M cases

6.4M cases

Practice Problem #12

Our client is a carpet manufacturer. They are launching a new, higher quality carpet for $20 per yard, which is a 25% premium over their standard carpet.

- 30% of their existing customers would upgrade to the new carpet and no longer purchase the standard carpet

- There is also a market of 70M yard per year that our client thinks they could capture 5% of with this new carpet

- Our client historically produces and sells 10M yards of carpet

Based on this information, by what percentage will their revenues increase by?

Solution to #12

Old revenue = 10M yards * ($20 / 1.25) = $160M

New revenue = (70% * $160M) + (30% * 10M * $20) + (70M * 5% * $20) = $242M

Percent change = ($242M - $160M) / $160M = 51.25%

Revenue will increase by 51.25%.

Practice Problem #13

Our client is considering entering the U.S. wireless market. How many subscribers would they need to cover their initial investment and annual fixed costs?

- The average subscriber remains a customer for 4 years

- The average subscriber uses 900 minutes a month

- Price per minute is $0.06

- The initial investment is $25M

- Annual fixed costs are $25M

- Per customer costs:

- Marketing: $114 (one-time cost)
- Sales commission = $50 (for 24-month contract)
- Average handsets purchased = 1 (every 24 months)
- Cost per handset = $200
- Cost per minute is $0.04

Solution to #13

Revenue per customer = 4 years * 12 months/year * 900 minutes a month * $0.06 = $2,592

Costs per customer = $114 + (2 * $50) + (2 * $200) + (4 years * 12 months/year * 900 minutes a month * $0.04) = $2,342

Profit per customer = $2,592 - $2,342 = $250

Subscribers to break even = [$25M + (4 * $25M)] / $250 = 500,000 subscribers

500,000 subscribers

Practice Problem #14

A friend is considering purchasing a yoga studio. The studio offers 100 classes per month at a price of $10 per class. The studio has monthly costs of $8,000.

<u>Part A</u>: What is the minimum average number of students per class needed to break even?

<u>Part B</u>: Last year, the studio had a loss of $24,000. By what percentage does the studio need to increase enrollment to break even?

Solution to #14

Part A

Let x = number of people per class

Revenue = 100 * $10 * x = $1,000x

Costs = $8,000

$1,000x = $8,000

x = 8

Each class needs to have an average of 8 people to break even.

Part B

Let's calculate the average number of students per class last year.

-24,000 / 12 = -2,000 per month

Let x = number of people per class

(100 * $10 * x) - $8,000 = -$2,000

x = 6 people per class

Percent change = (8 – 6) / 6 = 33% (rounded)

The studio needs to increase enrollment by 33% per class.

Practice Problem #15

Our client is a dry wall manufacturer and is concerned about a new low price player coming into the market. Our client is considering lowering its price by 10%.

Here is some information on our client:

- Number of units sold: 100,000

- Selling price per unit: $10

- Variable cost per unit: $3

- Fixed costs: $200,000

Part A: What would be the percent change in profit if they lowered prices? Assume that volume will remain the same with the price cut.

Part B: If our client maintains the same price, how much volume could they lose, as a percentage, to make it equivalent to cutting the price by 10%?

Solution to #15

Part A

Original profit = 100,000 * ($10 - $3) - $200,000 = $500,000

New profit = 100,000 * ($9 - $3) - $200,000 = $400,000

Percent change = ($400,000 - $500,000) / $500,000 = -20%

Profit will decrease by 20%.

Part B

Let the new volume of units the client sells = x

$10x - $3x - $200,000 = $400,000

$7x = $600,000

x = 85,714 units (rounded)

Percent change = (85,714 – 100,000) / 100,000 = -14.3% (rounded)

The client could lose 14.3% volume to make it equivalent to cutting the price by 10%.

Practice Problem #16

Organs will be harvested from terminally ill or injured patients just before death only if they are a registered organ donor or if the hospital receives permission from the next of kin.

If New York City expects to need 9,200 kidneys per year, what percent of New York City residents need to be registered donors to meet this goal?

Here is some additional information:

- New York City has a population of roughly 10 million

- The percentage of people that become terminally ill or injured each year is 0.1%

- The percentage of families that give consent to harvest organs is 10%

- Assume each donor has 2 kidneys

Solution to #16

Let x = the percent of New York City residents who are registered organ donors.

- Organs donated from registered donors = 10,000,000 * 0.1% * x * 2 = 20,000x

- Organs donated from non-registered donors that give consent = 10,000,000 * 0.1% * (1 – x) * 10% * 2 = 2,000 – 2000x

Let's set the sum of these two equal to 9,200 and solve for x.

20,000x + 2,000 − 2,000x = 9,200

18,000x = 7,200

x = 0.4

40% of New York City residents need to be registered organ donors.

Practice Problem #17

Your client is a U.S. storage company that rents out storage space at its own facilities. It is considering entering into the commercial portable storage market

Here's how it would work:

- Deliver the storage unit to companies
- Allow them to rent it for as long as they need to
- Pick up the container when they are done with it

Expected revenue details:

- 80% of storage units are utilized
- Average length of contract is 10 weeks
- Price is $300 per week
- Storage units are used all year (assume 50 weeks)

Expected cost details:

- 400 storage units are needed

- Storage units cost $15,000 each

- Average one-way transportation distance is 250 miles

- Cost per mile of transportation is $4

- Costs to store all of the storage units is $200,000 per year

- Overhead is $100,000 per year

What is the expected profit in the first year of operation?

Solution to #17

Let's calculate revenue first.

Revenue = 400 storage units * 80% utilization * 50 weeks * $300 per week = $4.8M

Let's calculate costs next.

- Storage unit costs = $15,000 * 400 = $6M

- Transportation costs = 2 * 250 * $4 * 400 * 80% * (50/10) = $3.2M

- Fixed costs = $200,000 + $100,000 = $300K

- Total costs = $6M + $3.2M + $300K = $9.5M

Profit = $4.8M - $9.5M = -$4.7M

The expected profit in the first year of operation is a loss of $4.7M.

Practice Problem #18

A factory needs 3 pounds of resin to produce 1 pound of rubber. 4 trains carrying resin that arrive at the factory in the beginning of every day. Their maximum capacity is:

- 10 carts per train
- 25 barrels of resin per cart
- 640 pounds of resin per barrel

Additionally, there are 2 trains that carry the finished rubber out of the factory at the end of the day and deliver it to a port. Their maximum capacity is:

- 8 carts per train
- 25 cases per cart
- 500 pounds of rubber per cart

How many pounds of rubber can this factory produce and deliver to a port each month? Assume the factory operates 25 days a month.

Solution to #18

We need to calculate the maximum capacity of the trains carrying in resin and the trains carrying out rubber to determine which is the bottleneck.

Trains carrying resin in:

Daily capacity: 4 trains * 10 carts per train * 25 barrels per cart * 640 pounds of resin per barrel * = 640,000 pounds of resin

Monthly capacity: 640,000 pounds of resin per day * 25 days = 16M pounds of resin

16M pounds of resin / 3 = 5.33M (rounded) pounds of rubber

Trains carrying rubber out:

Daily capacity: 2 trains * 8 carts per train * 25 cases per cart * 500 pounds rubber per cart = 200,000 pounds of rubber

Monthly capacity: 200,000 pounds of rubber per day * 25 days = 5M pounds of rubber

The bottleneck is the trains that carry rubber out of the factory. While the factory can produce 5.33M pounds of rubber a month, it can only deliver 5M pounds to the port in a month.

The factory can produce and deliver 5M pounds of rubber each month.

Practice Problem #19

An oil company is evaluating the purchase of one of three oil fields. Wells are dug by rigs. Once a well has been completed, the rig moves on to dig another well.

Wells are continuously dug for only one year and then oil is extracted going forward. Oil sells for $50 per barrel. Assume there are 360 days of operation in a year. Here is some information on the three oil fields:

	Oil Field A	Oil Field B	Oil Field C
Cost of rights to extract oil	$40M	$40M	$40M
# of rigs	10	10	10
Average well depth	1,200m	2,700m	3,600m
Average well production	100 barrels per day	200 barrels per day	300 barrels per day
Drilling rate	20m per day	30m per day	20m per day
Cost per rig per day	$5,000	$10,000	$20,000

Based on this information, which oil field has the highest profit during the first year of production? Remember that drilling happens in the first year and production begins in the second year.

Solution to #19

The first step is to calculate how many wells are drilled in each oil field in the first year.

- Oil Field A = (360 days * 10 rigs * 20m per day) / 1,200m = 60 wells

- Oil Field B = (360 days * 10 rigs * 30m per day) / 2,700m = 40 wells

- Oil Field C = (360 days * 10 rigs * 20m per day) / 3,600m = 20 wells

Next, we can calculate the revenue for each oil field in the first year of production.

- Oil Field A = 60 wells * 100 barrels per day * 360 days * $50 per barrel = $108M

- Oil Field B = 40 wells * 200 barrels per day * 360 days * $50 per barrel = $144M

- Oil Field C = 20 wells * 300 barrels per day * 360 days * $50 per barrel = $108M

Finally, we can calculate the profit for each oil field by subtracting the costs of the rights to extract oil and the costs of the rigs.

- Oil Field A = $108M - $40M - (10 rigs * $5,000 per rig per day * 360 days) = $50M

- Oil Field B = $144M - $40M - (10 rigs * $10,000 per rig per day * 360 days) = $68M

- Oil Field C = $108M − $40M − (10 rigs * $20,000 per rig per day * 360 days) = −$4M

Oil Field B has the highest profit during the first year of production at $68M.

Practice Problem #20

Our client is a for-profit specialty college. The CEO is considering investing in a new campus next year.

The costs to build the campus is $4.5M, which can be spread out evenly over a three-year period.

Here is some additional information on our client's current financials:

Client Financials	
Number of campuses	10
Student enrollments across all campuses	10,000
Total annual revenue from enrollments	$150,000,000
Total annual fixed costs	$48,000,000
Total annual variable costs	$80,000,000
Total annual operating profit	$22,000,000

How many students are required to enroll to break even in each of the first three years?

Solution to #20

Number of students to break even = (Build costs + Estimated fixed costs) / Profit per student

Build costs = $4.5M / 3 years = $1.5M

Estimated fixed costs = $48M / 10 campuses = $4.8M

Profit per student = ($150M - $80M) / 10,000 = $7K

Number of students to break even = ($1.5M + $4.8M) / $7K = 900

900 students are required to break even in each of the first three years.

Practice Problem #21

Our client offers afterschool programming focused on supporting at-risk youth in high school, enabling them to enter and succeed in college. At-risk youth are those who are at risk of dropping out due to poor grades or have already done so.

Our client is considering expanding into four regions. Here is some information on those regions:

	# of high schools	Average enrollment	% of students that drop out	% of non-dropouts with low grades
Region A	3	1,000	30%	30%
Region B	2	800	25%	25%
Region C	1	800	25%	20%
Region D	4	1,300	15%	20%

Which is the total number of students at-risk?

Solution to #21

At-risk youth consist of two segments, students that drop out and students that have low grades. Let's calculate the number of students that drop out in each region first.

- Region A = 3 * 1,000 * 30% = 900

- Region B = 2 * 800 * 25% = 400

- Region C = 1 * 800 * 25% = 200

- Region D = 4 * 1,300 * 15% = 780

Total drop-outs = 900 + 400 + 200 + 780 = 2,280

Next, let's calculate the number of students with low grades. The percentages given in the problem apply to non-dropouts.

- Region A = [(3 * 1,000) - 900] * 30% = 630

- Region B = [(2 * 800) - 400] * 25% = 300

- Region C = [(1 * 800) - 200] * 20% = 120

- Region D = [(4 * 1,300) - 780] * 20% = 884

Total students with low grades = 630 + 300 + 120 + 884 = 1,934

Finally, we can these to two segments to get our answer.

2,280 + 1,934 = 4,214

There are 4,214 students at-risk.

Practice Problem #22

A consumer electronics manufacturer is trying to determine the optimal price for their latest laptop to maximize revenue. Based on the chart below, what price should they set?

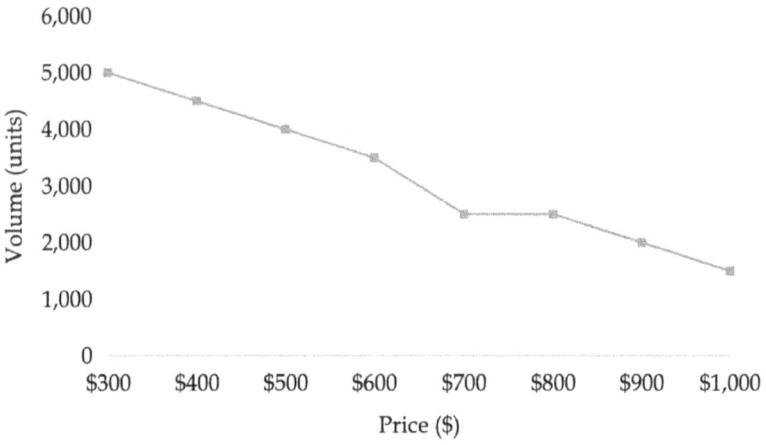

Solution to #22

Let's calculate the revenue at each price point

- $300: 5,000 * $300 = $1.5M
- $400: 4,500 * $400 = $1.8M
- $500: 4,000 * $500 = $2M
- $600: 3,500 * $600 = $2.1M
- $700: 2,500 * $700 = $1.75
- $800: 2,500 * $800 = $2M
- $900: 2,000 * $900 = $1.8M
- $1,000: 1,500 * $1,000 = $1.5M

The optimal price that maximizes revenue is $600, which would generate $2.1M.

Practice Problem #23

Our client is a manufacturer of remotely piloted aircraft. They currently sell one aircraft model called Falcon and sell 50 of them per year.

Our client is considering launching one of three new models. However, launching a new model will lead to fewer Falcon sales due to sales cannibalization.

Aircraft	New aircraft sales to Customer A	New aircraft sales to Customer B	Falcon sales lost due to cannibalization
Blue Jay	50	0	40%
Red Wing	0	60	70%
Black Hawk	38	52	90%

Aircraft	Price per aircraft
Falcon	$110,000
Blue Jay	$220,000
Red Wing	$210,000
Black Hawk	$180,000

Which product should our client launch to maximize revenue?

Solution to #23

Revenue is the sum of Falcon sales and the sales of the new aircraft.

Let's first calculate revenue from Falcon sales in each of the four scenarios: not launching a new product, launching Blue Jay, launching Red Wing, and launching Black Hawk.

- No product launch: 50 * $110,000 = $5.5M

- Blue Jay launch: 50 * $110,000 * (1 − 40%) = $3.3M

- Red Wing launch: 50 * $110,000 * (1 – 70%) = $1.65M

- Black Hawk launch: 50 * $110,000 * (1 – 90%) = $550K

Next, let's calculate revenue from the new aircraft that is launched.

- No product launch: $0

- Blue Jay launch: 50 * $220,000 = $11M

- Red Wing launch: 60 * $210,000 = $12.6M

- Black Hawk launch: 90 * $180,000 = $16.2M

We can add up Falcon sales and new aircraft sales to get total revenue in each of the four scenarios.

- No product launch: $5.5M + $0 = $5.5M

- Blue Jay launch: $3.3M + $11M = $14.3M

- Red Wing launch: $1.65M + $12.6M = $14.25M

- Black Hawk launch: $550K + $16.2M = $16.75M

Launching Black Hawk has the highest revenue at $16.75M.

Practice Problem #24

Our client is a major TV network that wants to know how much to bid on the TV rights for the upcoming Olympic Games.

There will be 16 days of programming:

- Opening Ceremony on a Friday from 8PM – 11PM

- 14 days of programming for 10 hours a day:

- Monday-Friday: 9AM - 12PM, 2PM - 5PM, 7PM - 11PM
- Saturday-Sunday: 11AM - 9PM

• Closing Ceremony on the following Saturday from 8PM – 11PM

There will be 10 minutes of advertising for every hour of programming.

- Ads during prime time generate $400K per 30 seconds
- Ads during non-prime time generate $200K per 30 seconds.

Prime Time is considered any time after 7PM on weekdays and all day during weekends.

Olympic programming will replace regularly scheduled programming. Ads during regular programming typically generate $1M per hour of programming.

What is the most that the major TV network should bid for broadcasting rights?

Solution to #24

First, let's calculate the number of hours of prime time and non-prime time.

- Prime time: $3 + (10 * 4) + (4 * 10) + 3 = 86$ hours
- Non-prime time: $10 * 6 = 60$ hours

Next, we'll calculate the minutes of ads.

- Prime time: $86 * 10 = 860$ minutes

- Non-prime time: 60 * 10 = 600 minutes

Afterwards, we'll calculate the ad revenue.

- Prime time revenue: 860 * $400K * 2 = $688M
- Non-prime time revenue: 600 * $200K * 2 = $240M
- Total revenue = $688M + $240M = $928M

Remember that the TV network would have generated revenue of $1M per hour with regularly scheduled programming during this time if they did not broadcast the Olympics.

Opportunity cost = (86 + 60) * $1M = $146M

Breakeven = $928M - $146M = $782M

The TV network should bid $782M at most.

Practice Problem #25

What is the annual profit made by residential household cleaning services in the U.S.?

Here is some information that you can use:

- There are 100M households in the U.S.
- 50% of households have a household income above $100K
- 50% of households have a household income below $100K
- 40% of households with income above $100K are willing to pay for cleaning services
- 10% of households with income below $100K are willing to pay for cleaning services

- The average price for a cleaning service is $75

- The average cleaning lasts 5 hours

- Cleaning labor costs are $10 per hour

- Cleaning supplies cost $5 per job

- Households schedule an average of 20 cleanings per year

Solution to #25

First, let's calculate the number of households that are willing to pay for cleaning services.

Households that pay for cleaning services = (100M * 50% * 40%) + (100M * 50% * 10%) = 25M

Next, let's calculate the profit per cleaning.

Profit per cleaning = $75 − (5 * $10) - $5 = $20

Finally, we can calculate the annual profit made by residential household cleaning services.

Annual profit = 25M households * 20 cleanings per year * $20 profit per cleaning = $10B

Annual profit is $10B.

Practice Problem #26

Our client is a top three beverage manufacturer in the U.S. They are thinking of launching a new flavored, non-sparkling water product.

Our client believes they can capture half the market share of the largest player in the flavored, non-sparking water market.

If there are 8M gallons of water sold in the entire flavored water market and one bottle contains 16 oz., how many bottles would our client need to sell each year?

As a reminder, 1 gallon is equal to 128 oz.

Here is some information on the market:

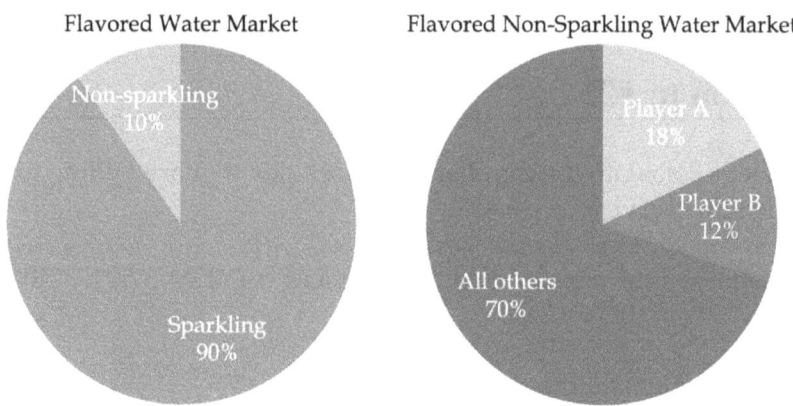

Solution to #26

Flavored non-sparkling water market = 10% * 8M gallons = 800,000 gallons

800,000 gallons * 128 oz. / 16oz. = 6.4M bottles

6.4M bottles * (18% / 2) = 576,000 bottles

576,000 bottles

Practice Problem #27

A major bank is looking for new card member growth in the United States. They want to target the Hispanic market because their penetration is low compared to competitors.

<u>Part A</u>: The bank has set a goal of achieving 30% market share among the addressable Hispanic market. How much is this additional market share worth?

Here is some further information on the market:

- There are 40M Hispanic people in the U.S.

- 3/8 of them are too young to have credit cards and are excluded from the addressable market

- The bank currently has 10% market share among the addressable Hispanic market

- The average customer is worth $160 to the bank over the course of their life

- The average Hispanic customer is worth 25% more than the average customer

<u>Part B</u>: The bank uses direct mail campaigns to acquire new card members. Here is some information on these campaigns:

- The average response rate for Hispanic prospects is 4%

- The bank is planning to target 15M potential customers with 3 mailings this year

- After the first mailing, the response rate will drop by 50% in each of the following mailings

- The bank has a conversion rate of 50% of respondents

How many new customers should the bank expect this year?

Solution to #27

Part A

Let's first calculate how many additional Hispanic customers the bank needs.

Addressable Hispanic customers = 40M * (5/8) = 25M

Number of additional customers needed = 25M * (30% - 10%) = 5M

Next, let's calculate how much these additional customers are worth.

Revenue = 5M * ($160 * 1.25) = $1B

The additional market share is worth $1B.

Part B

Let's calculate the number of respondents.

First mailing = 15M * 4% = 600,000 respondents

Second mailing = 15M * 4% / 2 = 300,000 respondents

Third mailing = 15M * 4% / 2 / 2 = 150,000 respondents

Total respondents = 600,000 + 300,000 + 150,000 = 1,050,000

Next, let's calculate the number of new customers.

New customers = 1,050,000 * 50% = 525,000

The bank will acquire 525,000 new customers.

Practice Problem #28

Our client is a U.S. airline with a popular frequent flyer mile program. They sell frequent flyer miles through partnerships with rental car agencies.

These agencies will advertise that customers can get a certain number of frequent flier miles per car rental day. When customers request frequent flier miles, they get the miles and the agency pays the airline for the transaction.

Here is some information on the program:

- There are 5 rental car agency partners

- There is a total of 10M rentals per year by our frequent flier members

- The average price per day of car rental is $45

- The average car rental is for 3 days

- Car rental agencies have a 10% profit margin on car rentals before paying for any frequent flier miles

- Current payments from rental car agencies to our client is $3 per transaction

Part A: How much money does the average rental car agency partner make?

Part B: Our client is considering making the partnerships with rental car agencies more exclusive. They will cut the number of partners from 5 down to 3.

To be a part of this exclusive partnership, rental car agencies would need to pay an upfront partnership fee for the year.

How much would rental car agencies be willing to pay to participate in this exclusive partnership program?

Assume that the client's frequent flier members will only rent a car from a rental car agency that is a partner. Also assume that it still costs rental car agencies $3 per transaction.

Solution to #28

Part A

10M rentals per year / 5 rental car agencies = 2M rentals per rental car agency

Profit per transaction = ($45 * 3 * 10%) - $3 = $10.5

Profit per rental car agency = 2M * $10.5 = $21M

The average rental car agency makes $21M.

Part B

Let's calculate the new profit under this more exclusive partnership.

Profit per transaction stays the same, but the number of transactions increases.

Profit per rental car agency = (10M / 3) * $10.5 = $35M

The average rental car agency makes $35M now, an increase from the $21M it was making previously.

$35M - $21M = $14M

Rental car agencies would be willing to pay up to $14M to participate in this exclusive partnership program.

Practice Problem #29

A movie theater offers customers three different subscription plans to watch movies:

- Plan A: $75 per year to watch 1 movie per month

- Plan B: $100 per year to watch 2 movies per month

- Plan C: $200 per year to watch 5 movies per month

Assuming that customers fully utilized their subscription, which movie theater had the highest number of customer visits last year?

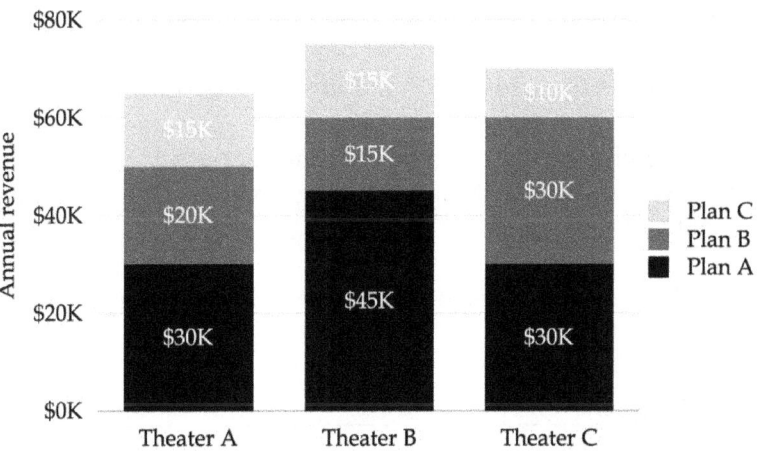

Solution to #29

Let's calculate the number of visits in each theater.

- Theater A: ($30K / $75 * 1) + ($20K / $100 * 2) + ($15K / $200 * 5) = 1,175 visits

- Theater B: ($45K / $75 * 1) + ($15K / $100 * 2) + ($15K / $200 * 5) = 1,275 visits

- Theater C: ($30K / $75 * 1) + ($30K / $100 * 2) + ($10K / $200 * 5) = 1,250 visits

Theater B had the most visits with 1,275.

Practice Problem #30

Our client manufactures industrial tools and machinery with an annual revenue of $1B and a profit margin of 5%.

70% of revenues come from the Tools product line and 30% of revenues come from the Machinery product line.

In the Tools product line, they have 20% market share and in the Machinery product line, they have 40% market share.

Part A: What is the size of each market?

Part B: Our client is considering moving manufacturing of the Tools product line to China. Manufacturing costs for the Tools product line is 80% of its revenue.

If our client makes this move, what will be their overall profit margin?

Cost component	U.S.	China
Materials	50% of cost	50% of U.S. cost
Labor	20% of cost	90% cheaper than U.S.
Freight	10% of cost	3x price of U.S.
Overhead	20% of cost	Same as U.S.

Solution to #30

Part A

Tool revenue = 70% * $1B = $700M

Tool market size = $700M / 20% = $3.5B

Machinery revenue = 30% * $1B = $300M

Machinery market size = $300M / 40% = $750M

The Tool market size is $3.5B and the Machinery market size is $750M.

Part B

Let's first calculate the manufacturing costs for the Tool product line.

Tools manufacturing costs = ($1B * 70%) * (80%) = $560M

Next, we can calculate the cost of each component in the U.S.

- Materials: $560M * 50% = $280M

- Labor: $560M * 20% = $112M

- Freight: $560M * 10% = $56M

- Overhead: $560M * 20% = $112M

- Total costs: $560M

Afterwards, let's calculate the cost of each component in China

- Materials: $280M * 50% = $140M

- Labor: $112M * (1 - 90%) = $11.2M

- Freight: $56M * 3 = $168M

- Overhead: $112M

- Total costs: $140M + $11.2M + $168M + $112M = $431.2M

Cost savings = $560M - $431.2 = $128.8M

The company currently has a profit margin of 5% or a profit of $1B * 5% = $50M. All of the cost savings from moving manufacturing to China directly increase profit.

New profit margin = ($50M + $128.8M) / $1B = 17.88%

The new overall profit margin is 17.88%.

Practice Problem #31

What is the number of recreational airplanes purchased in the U.S. each year? Here are some assumptions that you can make:

- There are 300M people in the U.S.
- 1% of the population has a pilot's license
- 1/3 of those with a pilot's license has enough income to own a plane or part of a plane
- Of those that can afford to own a plane or part of a plane, 10% buy their own plane
- The remainder of those that can afford to own a plane or part of a plane belong to flying clubs
- In a flying club, ownership of a plane is shared by 10 pilots
- Planes have a useful life of 20 years

Solution to #31

300M people * 1% = 3M people with a pilot's license

3M * 1/3 = 1M people with a pilot's license with high income

1M * 10% = 100K planes purchased

(1M − 100K) / 10 = 90K planes purchased through flying clubs

100K + 90K = 190K total planes purchased

190K / 20 = 9,500 planes purchased each year

There are 9,500 recreational planes purchased each year.

Practice Problem #32

Our client is a health insurance company that is working on developing their strategic plan for the next 5-10 years. The Board of Directors has brainstormed a list of several different potential initiatives. However, they don't have the resources to do all of them.

The CEO and CFO have each given a score of 1-5 across several different goals of the company. A score of 5 indicates that the initiative is a strong fit for the goal. A score of 1 indicates that the initiative is a weak fit for the goal.

Goal 1 is twice as important as Goal 2. It is also twice as important as Goal 3. Goal 2 and Goal 3 are about the same level of importance.

The CEO's opinion is also twice as important as the CFO.

Here are the scorecards:

CEO's Scorecard:

Initiative	Goal 1	Goal 2	Goal 3
A	3	4	5
B	4	3	5
C	5	2	2
D	3.5	5	5

CFO's Scorecard:

Initiative	Goal 1	Goal 2	Goal 3
A	3	5	5
B	4	3	3
C	5	1	2
D	4	4	2

Which initiative should our client focus on?

Solution to #32

Let's add up the points for each initiative for each scorecard. We'll need to double the value of points for Goal 1 since it is twice as important as Goal 2 or Goal 3.

CEO Scorecard:

- A: (3 * 2) + 4 + 5 = 15
- B: (4 * 2) + 3 + 5 = 16
- C: (5 * 2) + 2 + 2 = 14
- D: (3.5 * 2) + 5 + 5 = 17

CFO Scorecard:

- A: (3 * 2) + 5 + 5 = 16
- B: (4 * 2) + 3 + 3 = 14
- C: (5 * 2) + 1 + 2 = 13
- D: (4 * 2) + 4 + 2 = 14

Now, we can add up the scores from the two scorecards. We'll need to double the value of points from the CEO scorecard since the CEO's opinion is twice as important as the CFO.

- A: (15 * 2) + 16 = 46
- B: (16 * 2) + 14 = 46
- C: (14 * 2) + 13 = 41
- D: (17 * 2) + 14 = 48

Our client should focus on Initiative D, which has the highest adjusted total score.

Practice Problem #33

Our client produces golf clubs in the U.S. They expect demand for a new golf club they are launching to be 60,000 sets per year. They are deciding whether to build a new plant or expand the current plant.

Building a new plant:

- Initial one-time investment of $2M
- Two types of machines are available:
  - Machine Type A: Produces 2,000 sets per month and costs $12.5M
  - Machine Type B: Produces 1,250 sets per month and costs $8M
- The new plant can only have 3 machines operating

Expanding the current plant:

- Initial one-time investment of $2M

- Two types of machines are available:

    - Machine Type A: Produces 1,250 sets per month and costs $8M

    - Machine Type B: Produces 7,500 sets per year and costs $5.5M

Part A: If building a new plant, what is the lowest possible cost to manufacture at least 60,000 sets per year?

Part B: If expanding the current plant, what is the lowest possible cost to manufacture at least 60,000 sets per year?

Solution to #33

Part A

Let's calculate how much each machine type produces per year:

- Machine Type A: 2,000 * 12 = 24,000 sets per year

- Machine Type B: 1,250 * 12 = 15,000 sets per year

Since we can only have 3 machines operating, we can reach at least 60,000 sets by either having:

- 3 Type A

- 2 Type A and 1 Type B

It would require 4 Type B machines to reach 60,000 sets, which is not possible given that we can only have 3 machines operating.

Since Type B costs less than Type A, the lowest cost solution is 2 Type A and 1 Type B.

This would produce 24,000 + 24,000 + 15,000 = 63,000 sets per year.

Cost = $12.5M + $12.5M + $8M + $2M initial investment = $35M

$35M

Part B

Let's calculate how much each machine type produces per year:

- Machine Type A: 1,250 * 12 = 15,000 sets per year

- Machine Type B: 7,500 sets per year

Given that Type A produces twice the number of sets but at less than twice the cost of Type B, Type A is the more cost-effective option.

We would need 4 Type A machines to produce 60,000 sets per year.

Cost = (4 * $8M) + $2M initial investment = $34M

$34M

Practice Problem #34

A burger franchise in a small town is open for lunch and dinner. Lunch makes up 60% of their revenue while dinner makes up 40%. They make an average profit of $10 per customer with a 50% profit margin.

Part A: If the average profit for a lunch customer is $8 per customer, what is the average profit for a dinner customer?

Part B: A nearby competitor has 20% higher revenues and 10% higher costs. What is their average profit per customer?

Solution to #34

Part A

Let x = average profit for a dinner customer

(0.6 * $8) + (0.4 * x) = $10

x = $13

The average profit per dinner customer is $13.

Part B

Competitor revenue per customer = 1.2 * ($10 / 50%) = $24

Competitor cost per customer = 1.1 * ($20 - $10) = $11

Competitor profit per customer = $24 - $11 = $13

The competitor's average profit per customer is $13.

Practice Problem #35

A large beverage company has five different product lines. Based on the charts below, what is the percent change in sales from last year to this year?

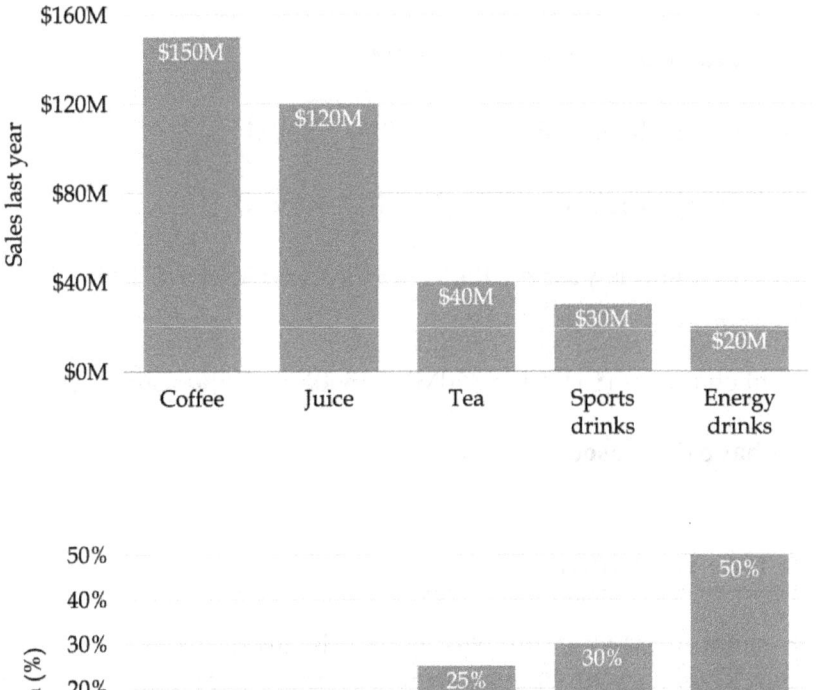

Solution to #35

Total revenue last year = $150M + $120M + $40M + $30M + $20M = $360M

Revenue this year:

- Coffee: $150M * (1 − 20%) = $120M

- Juice: $120M * (1 - 10\%) = \$108M$

- Tea: $40M * (1 + 25\%) = \$50M$

- Sports drinks: $30M * (1 + 30\%) = \$39M$

- Energy drinks: $20M * (1 + 50\%) = \$30M$

Total revenue this year = $120M + $108M + $50M + $39M + $30M = $347M

Percent change = ($347M - $360M) / $360M = 3.6% (rounded)

Sales have decreased by 3.6%.

Practice Problem #36

Our client produces the plastic that is used for making plastic bottles. They currently have a factory in the U.S. and are considering purchasing another factory in Europe to be closer to their customers.

Here is some information:

- The cost of purchasing the factory is $750M

- Plant costs are $800M and will be spread out evenly over 50 years

- The plant has a capacity of 1M tons per year

- The current price of plastic is $920 per ton

- Raw material costs are $690 per ton

- Energy costs are $30 per ton

- Overhead and logistics costs are $80M per year

The factory would provide two synergies to our client:

- Overhead savings of $20M per year
- Logistics savings of $20 per ton

Part A: What is the payback period?

Part B: If the price of plastic drops to $800 per ton, what would the payback period be?

Solution to #36

Part A

Annual profit = 1M * ($920 - $690 - $30 + $20) − ($800M/50) - $80M + $20M = $144M

Payback period = $750M / $144M = 5.2 (rounded)

The payback period is roughly 5.2 years.

Part B

Annual profit = 1M * ($800 - $690 - $30 + $20) − ($800M/50) - $80M + $20M = $24M

Payback period = $750M / $24M = 31.25 years

The new payback period would be 31.25 years.

Practice Problem #37

Your client is a candy manufacturing company with a profit margin of 10%. They are facing declining profit margins.

Part A: A major competitor has prices that are 10% lower than our client's prices. The competitor's costs are 20% lower as well. What is their profit margin?

Part B: Our client's costs are 70% raw materials, 20% equipment, and 10% labor. If they want to have the same profit margin as their competitor, by what percentage do raw material costs need to decrease by?

Solution to #37

Part A

To make the math easier, let's set our client's price to $100. A 10% profit margin means that costs are $90.

Competitor's price = $100 * 0.9 = $90

Competitor's costs = $90 * 0.8 = $72

Competitor's profit margin = ($90 - $72) / $90 = 20%

20% profit margin

Part B

To make the math easier, let's continue to set our client's price to $100.

To reach the same profit margin as our competitor, costs need to decrease from $90 to $80. So, raw material costs need to decrease by $10.

Current raw material costs = 0.7 * $90 = $63

New raw material costs = $63 - $10 = $53

Percent change = ($53 - $63) / $63 = -15.9% (rounded)

Raw material costs need to decrease by 15.9%.

Practice Problem #38

Your client is a software company that makes photo editing, web design, video editing, and desktop publishing software.

Based on the chart below, what is their overall market share in all the markets that they sell in?

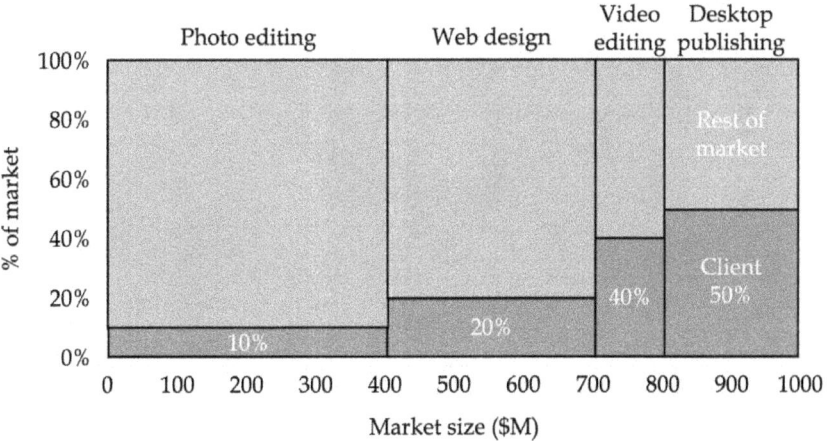

Solution to #38

Total market size = $1,000M

Client revenue = ($400M * 10%) + ($300M * 20%) + ($100M * 40%) + ($200M * 50%) = $240M

Market share = $240M / $1,000M = 24%

They have an overall market share of 24%.

Practice Problem #39

A pharmaceutical company is evaluating what drugs it should prioritize in its pipeline next year. It only wants to invest in drugs that are top 25% candidates.

Based on the chart below, what is the total market size of the drugs that are top 25% candidates?

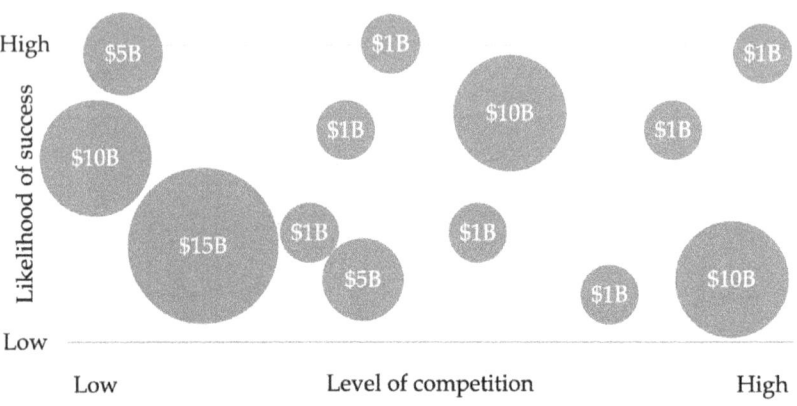

Solution to #39

We want to find drug candidates that have a high likelihood of success and low competition. This area is the top left quadrant of the bubble chart.

Market size = $10B + $5B + $1B + $1B = $17B

The top 25% drug candidates have a total market size of $17B.

Practice Problem #40

Your client is a mining company that has just purchased a mountain that has high concentrations of a valuable metal ore.

However, the mountain is made up of a hard type of rock and requires engineers to build a special type of drill that can be used to extract the metal from the mountain.

Your client is deciding whether to manufacture the drill in-house or outsource drill production:

- Manufacture in-house: There will be $30M in fixed setup costs and a variable cost of $100,000 per drill. Each drill will be able to mine 500 tons of ore per year and last 4 years

- Outsource drill production: Each drill will cost $250,000 but there will be no setup cost. Each drill will be able to mine 400 tons of ore per year and last for 2.5 years

The client will be mining the ore for 20 years. They are concerned about flooding the market with the mined ore, so will cap annual extraction based on the following schedule:

- Year 1-5: 10% of total U.S. production

- Year 6-10: 15% of total U.S. production

- Year 11-15: 20% of total U.S. production

- Year 16-20: 25% of total U.S. production

The annual U.S. production is 64,000 tons.

For logistical reasons, the client must also cap annual extraction to 12,000 tons in any given year.

Each ton of ore that is mined generates $325. Your client has $1M in operating costs per year.

What is the expected profit if they manufacture the drill-in house vs. outsource drill production?

Solution to #40

Let's first calculate the total tons that will be mined.

- Year 1-5: 10% * 64,000 = 6,400 tons per year

- Year 6-10: 15% * 64,000 = 9,600 tons per year

- Year 11-15: 20% * 64,000 = 12,800 tons per year, but the client is constrained to a maximum of 12,000 tons

- Year 16-20: 25% * 64,000 = 16,000 tons per year, but the client is constrained to a maximum of 12,000 tons

Total tons = (6,400 * 5) + (9,600 * 5) + (12,000 * 10) = 200,000 tons

Let's calculate the revenue from mining.

Revenue = 200,000 * 325 = $65M

Next, let's calculate the number of drills needed.

- Manufacturing in-house: 200,000 tons / (4 years per drill * 500 tons per drill per year) = 100 drills

- Outsourcing: 200,000 tons / (2.5 years per drill * 400 tons per drill per year) = 200 drills

Let's calculate the costs of drills in both scenarios.

- Drill costs if manufacturing in-house: $30M + ($100,000 * 100) = $40M

- Drill costs if outsource: $250,000 * 200 = $50M

Finally, we can calculate profit. Remember that we also need to include operating costs into our profit formula.

- Profit if manufacturing in-house = $65M - $40M - (20 years * $1M) = $5M profit

- Profit if outsourcing = $65M - $50M - (20 years * $1M) = $5M loss

Manufacturing the drill in-house will generate $5M in profit while outsourcing will result in a loss of $5M.

Practice Problem #41

A major airline is considering stopping accepting cash for in-flight food and beverage services. They would only accept major credit cards.

If they do this, roughly 1 in 3 customers that would purchase in-flight food and beverage services with cash will no longer purchase anything.

How much would revenue decrease by if they implemented this?

Here is some additional information:

- An airplane has 200 total seats

- Currently, 20% of in-flight purchases are paid in cash and 80% are paid with card

	% of Seats	Occupancy	% Business	% Leisure
First Class	25%	100%	100%	0%
Economy	75%	80%	50%	50%

	% that Purchase Food or Beverage	Average Spend
Business	75%	$10
Leisure	25%	$5

*Note: First Class travelers receive free food and beverage

Solution to #41

First, let's calculate the number of people in first class and economy.

- First class = 200 * 25% * 100% = 50 people

- Economy = 200 * 75% * 80% = 120 people

Next, let's calculate how many of these passengers are business and leisure.

- First class business = 50 * 100% = 50 people

- First class leisure = 50 * 0% = 0 people

- Economy business = 120 * 50% = 60 people

- Economy leisure = 120 * 50% = 60 people

Afterwards, we'll calculate how much is spent on in-flight food and beverage services.

- First class business = $0 (they receive free food and beverage)

- First class leisure = $0 (they receive free food and beverage)

- Economy business = 60 * 75% * $10 = $450

- Economy leisure = 60 * 25% * $5 = $75

Total spending per airplane is $450 + $75 = $525.

Finally, we can calculate how much revenue would be lost if cash is no longer accepted.

Revenue loss = $525 * 20% * (1/3) = $35

Revenue per airplane would decrease by $35.

Practice Problem #42

Our client is a leading provider of IT networking equipment with annual revenue of $20B and a profit margin of 25%. They have identified four different options to increase sales, but they only have the capacity to do one.

	Up-front costs	Good economy	Bad economy
Rewards program	$50M	5% increase in revenue	1% increase in revenue
Advertising campaign	$100M	10% increase in revenue	No effect
Hire key account representatives	$1M	1% increase in revenue	1% increase in revenue
Create special sales force	$25M	10% increase in revenue	5% decrease in revenue

Assume that there is a 50% chance of a good economy and a 50% chance of a bad economy.

Part A: Which option has the highest expected increase in profit?

Part B: Which option has the highest expected ROI?

Solution to #42

Part A

The first step is to calculate the impact on revenue in a good economy and in a bad economy for each option.

	Up-front costs	Good economy	Bad economy
Rewards program	$50M	+$1B revenue	+$200M revenue
Advertising campaign	$100M	+$2B revenue	No effect
Hire key account representatives	$1M	+$200M revenue	+$200M revenue
Create special sales force	$25M	+$2B revenue	-$1B revenue

The company has a 25% profit margin, so let's calculate the impact on profit.

	Up-front costs	Good economy	Bad economy
Rewards program	$50M	+$250M profit	+$50M profit
Advertising campaign	$100M	+$500M profit	No effect
Hire key account representatives	$1M	+$50M profit	+$50M profit
Create special sales force	$25M	+$500M profit	-$250M profit

Next, we can calculate the expected value change in profit for each of the four options and subtract the up-front costs.

- Rewards program = (50% * $250M) + (50% * $50M) - $50M = $100M

- Advertising = (50% * $500M) + (50% * $0) - $100M = $150M

- Key account reps = (50% * $50M) + (50% * $50M) - $1M = $49M

- Special sales force = (50% * $500M) + (50% * -$250M) - $25M = $100M

Advertising has the highest expected increase in profit of $150M.

Part B

Finally, we can calculate the ROI for each of the four options

- Rewards program = $100M / $50M = 200%

- Advertising = $150M / $100M = 150%

- Key account reps = $49M / $1M = 4,900%

- Special sales force = $100M / $25M = 400%

Hiring key account representatives has the highest expected ROI of 4,900%.

Practice Problem #43

A toy factory is trying to determine how much money is wasted from not reaching maximum worker utilization during the work day. The factory has 100 workers that are paid an average of $60,000 per year and work from 8AM to 6PM.

Based on the chart below, how much money is wasted each year due to lower than maximum worker utilization?

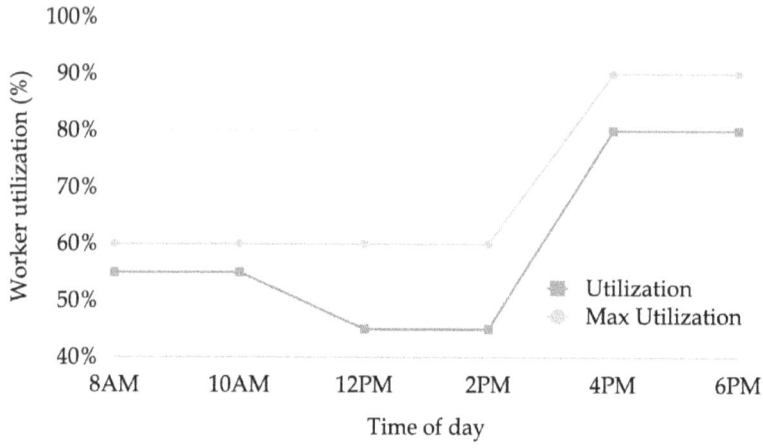

Solution to #43

We need to calculate the number of worker-equivalents that are not being utilized in each 2-hour segment.

- 8AM to 10AM: (60% - 55%) * 100 workers = 5 workers not utilized

- 10AM to 12PM: [(60% - 55%) + (60% - 45%)] / 2 * 100 workers = 10 workers not utilized

- 12PM to 2PM: (60% - 45%) * 100 = 15 workers not utilized

- 2PM to 4PM: [(60% - 45%) + (90% - 80%)] / 2 * 100 workers = 12.5 workers not utilized

- 4PM to 6PM: (90% - 80%) * 100 = 10 workers not utilized

Note that for 10AM to 12PM and 2PM to 4PM, we had to take the average of the difference in utilization at the start and end point since the difference in utilization changes over these periods.

Next, let's calculate the average across the entire day.

Average workers not utilized = (5 + 10 + 15 + 12.5 + 10) / 5 = 10.5 workers

Finally, let's calculate the dollar value of this.

10.5 workers * $60,000 per year = $630,000

$630,000 is wasted each year.

Practice Problem #44

A large retail chain is considering adding self-checkout stations to their stores to replace some of their cashiers. Assume that one self-checkout station can replace one cashier.

What are the expected annual savings in the first year?

Here is some information on the retail chain:

- There are 900 stores

- The average store has 16 cashiers per shift

- Stores operate on two shifts: 8AM – 4PM and 4PM to 12AM

- Cashiers make $10 per hour and work 8 hours per day

- Each self-checkout machine costs $40,000, including installation

- Assume self-checkout machine maintenance costs are negligible

- One employee can oversee 4 self-checkout machines

- Stores are open 350 days per year

Here is some information on customers:

- 10% of customers would not use the self-checkout machines and would prefer to shop elsewhere if forced to do so

- When a customer has more than 15 items, they prefer a cashier over self-checkout stations

- Customers have more than 15 items about 15% of the time

Solution to #44

Let's first calculate the number of machines needed in a single store. Since 10% + 15% = 25% of customers prefer cashiers, 25% of the cashiers must be retained.

Therefore, 75% of the cashiers can be replaced with machines.

75% * 16 cashiers = 12 machines needed

Operating 12 machines requires 12 / 4 = 3 employees.

In a single store, we are replacing 12 employees with 12 machines and 3 employees. So, we are effectively saving 9 employees.

Employee savings per day = 2 shifts * 9 employees * 8 hours per day * $10 per hour = $1,440

Employee savings per year = $1,440 * 350 = $504K

Machine costs = 12 * $40,000 = $480K

Net savings = $504K - $480K = $24K

Finally, multiply this annual savings per store by the number of stores.

$24K * 900 = $21.6M

The retail chain will save $21.6M in its first year.

Practice Problem #45

A drug manufacturer invented a new drug to treat depression. Unlike most antidepressants, the drug is preventative, designed for consumption before symptoms emerge.

Would insurance companies want to cover this drug? Assume that they would cover this drug if it saves them money.

Use the following information:

- There are 300M people in the U.S.

- 1 in 200 Americans suffer from depression

- Annual treatment for depression costs insurers $10,000 per person

- 1 in 100 Americans are at risk for depression and within that group, 1 in 5 are considered high risk for depression

- The new drug is targeted for those that are considered high risk for depression

- The new drug is taken on a daily basis for 365 days a year

- The new drug costs $50 per package, which contains 10 pills

- The new drug is 70% effective, which would save the person from the annual treatment costs for depression

- For the 30% of the time the drug is ineffective, the person will still require treatment for depression

Solution to #45

To determine whether insurance companies would cover this drug, let's first calculate how much they are currently paying for treatments for depression.

Current costs to insurers = 300M people * (1/200 suffer from depression) * $10,000 per person = $15B

Next, let's calculate how much it would cost to pay for this drug.

Drug costs = 300M * (1/100) * (1/5) * ($50/10 pills) * 365 = $1.095B

Remember that this drug is 70% effective, so 30% of people taking this drug will still need to receive treatment for depression.

Costs of treating ineffective cases = 300M * (1/100) * (1/5) * 30% * $10,000 = $1.8B

Lastly, remember that while there are 1.5M cases of depression, only 600K people are identified as high risk to take this drug. That leaves 900K people that would develop depression because they weren't identified as high risk.

Costs of treating those not identified as high risk = 900K * $10,000 = $9B

Finally, we can add up all of the costs to determine how much insurance companies would pay with this new drug to prevent and treat depression.

New costs = $1.095B + $1.8B + $9B = $11.895B

Insurance companies would cover this drug because it would cost them $11.895B instead of the $15B they currently pay to treat depression.

Practice Problem #46

Our client is a large media company. They currently have two offices in two different cities in California, Cupertino and Palo Alto. They have decided to combine operations into one building and will choose one of their existing buildings to build out and move into.

Based on the information below, which building should they pick?

- The client requires 100,000 square feet of space

- The client can rent out any space it doesn't use to other companies (charge for a sub-lease)

- The remaining time on both leases is 10 years

	Cupertino, CA	Palo Alto, CA
Space (sq. ft.)	200,000	400,000
Cost / sq. ft. / year	$40	$40
Build-out cost (over 10 years)	$15,000,000	$5,000,000
Average vacancy rate in the city	10%	18%
Sub-lease income	$40 / sq. ft. / year	$30 sq. ft. / year

Solution to #46

Let's calculate the impact on profit per year in the two different scenarios.

Build out and move into Cupertino, CA:

Costs

- Cupertino rent = 200,000 * $40 = $8M

- Palo Alto rent = 400,000 * $40 = $16M

- Cupertino build-out cost = $15,000,000 / 10 = $1.5M
- Total annual costs = $8M + $16M + $1.5M = $25.5M

Revenue

- Cupertino sub-lease income = (200,000 − 100,000) * $40 = $4M
- Palo Alto sub-lease income = 400,000 * $30 = $12M
- Total annual sub-lease income = $4M + $12M = $16M

Annual profit = $16M - $25.5M = -$9.5M

Build out and move into Palo Alto, CA:

Costs

- Cupertino rent = 200,000 * $40 = $8M
- Palo Alto rent = 400,000 * $40 = $16M
- Palo Alto build-out cost = $5,000,000 / 10 = $500K
- Total annual costs = $8M + $16M + $500K = $24.5M

Revenue

- Cupertino sub-lease income = 200,000 * $40 = $8M
- Palo Alto sub-lease income = (400,000 − 100,000) * $30 = $9M
- Total annual sub-lease income = $8M + $9M = $17M

Annual profit = $17M - $24.5M = -$7.5M

Moving into Palo Alto is the better choice. It would result in a loss of $7.5M per year instead of a loss of $9.5M from moving into Cupertino.

Practice Problem #47

Our client is a small maker of coffins in Croatia. There has been quite a lot of technological innovation in the market, causing them to lose market share. They are considering three options:

- Sell the business to a third party

- Sell the assets of the company and shut it down

- Invest in new technology and continue operating the business

<u>Part A</u>: Based on the information below, what is the current value of the company?

- The population of Croatia is 4M

- The population growth is 0%, the average life expectancy is 80 years, and there is an even distribution of ages

- 80% of people are buried in coffins

- Our client has a 10% market share

- Coffins are priced at $5,000

- Material costs are $480 and labor costs are $4,320

- Fixed costs for the business are $700,000 per year

- The company can be valued at 10 times its annual profit

<u>Part B</u>: Based on the information below, estimate roughly how much the client's land is worth.

- Purchase price of land: $100,000

- Years owned: 48

- Average real estate appreciation: 6% per year

Part C: Based on the information below, what is the annual profit of the company if they invest in new technology?

- The new technology will reduce labor costs by 25%

- The new technology costs $4M per year over the technology's lifetime

Solution to #47

Part A

Since the population growth is 0% and there is an even distribution of ages, 1/80 of the population dies each year.

Coffins sold per year = 4M * (1/80) * 80% * 10% market share = 4,000

Profit = [4,000 * ($5,000 - $480 - $4,320)] - $700,000 = $100,000 per year

Valuation = 10 * $100,000 = $1M

The company is currently valued at $1M.

Part B

We can use the Rule of 72 to estimate the current value of the land.

72 / 6 = 12 years

The Rule of 72 tells us that it takes roughly 12 years for the value of the land to double. Over 48 years, the value of the land doubles 48 / 12 = 4 times.

Value of land = $100,000 * 2 * 2 * 2 * 2 = $1,600,000

The land is worth $1.6M.

Part C

New labor cost = $4,320 * 75\% = $3,240

Profit = [4,000 * ($5,000 - $480 - $3,240)] - $700,000 - $4,000,000 = $420,000 per year

With the new technology, annual profit is $420,000 per year.

Practice Problem #48

Our client services commercial vehicles. 70% of their revenue comes from parts and 30% of their revenue comes from services. Parts have an average profit margin of 4% while services have an average profit margin of 15%.

A major competitor has 60% of revenue coming from parts and 40% of revenue coming from services. Their profit margins are 5% for parts and 15% for services.

Part A: What are the overall profit margins for our client and their major competitor?

Part B: What percentage of this difference is caused by product mix versus a lower profit margin for parts?

Solution to #48

Part A

Client profit margin = (70% * 4%) + (30% * 15%) = 7.3%

Competitor profit margin = (60% * 5%) + (40% * 15%) = 9%

Our client has a profit margin of 7.3% while our competitor has a profit margin of 9%.

Part B

Let's calculate our client's profit margin if they had the same product mix as their competitor.

Client profit margin (with same product mix) = (60% * 4%) + (40% * 15%) = 8.4%

Next, let's calculate our client's profit margin if they had the same parts profit margin as the competitor.

Client profit margin (with same parts margin) = (70% * 5%) + (30% * 15%) = 8%

Changing only the product mix increases profit margin by 8.4% - 7.3% = 1.1%. Changing only the parts profit margin increases profit margin by 8% - 7.3% = 0.7%.

We can calculate the percentage difference in profit margin versus the competitor that is caused by these two drivers.

Product mix = 1.1% / (1.1% + 0.7%) = 61% (rounded)

Parts margin = 0.7% / (1.1% + 0.7%) = 39% (rounded)

61% of the profit margin difference is due to product mix while 39% of the difference is due to the lower profit margin of parts.

Practice Problem #49

Our client is a major hotel chain that is considering acquiring an existing hotel in Miami for $20M. Their goal is to get an ROI of 20% over three years. Should they make the investment?

Here is some information:

- On weekends, Miami has 6,000 visitors a day and 5% stay in the hotel

- Group room rates are $120 per night
- Individual room rates are $150 per night
- On weekends, 75% of guests pay individual room rates and the remainder pay group room rates
- On weekdays, 40% of guests pay individual room rates and the remainder pay group room rates
- Weekend hotel occupancy rate is 60%
- Weekday hotel occupancy rate is 75%
- It costs the hotel $30 per room per night for each occupied room
- Fixed costs for the hotel are $5,750 per night
- Assume the hotel operates for 52 weeks per year

Solution to #49

Let's calculate the profit for a weekend day.

Weekend profit per room = (0.75 * $150) + (0.25 * $120) - $30 = $112.5

Number of weekend guests = 6,000 * 5% = 300

Weekend profit per day = $112.5 * 300 = $33,750

Next, let's calculate the profit for a weekday.

We know that 300 guests on the weekend is equal to a 60% occupancy rate. So, we can calculate how many guests is equal to a 75% occupancy rate on a weekday.

300 / 60% = x / 75%

x = 375 guests on a weekday

Weekday profit per guest = (0.4 * $150) + (0.6 * $120) - $30 = $102

Weekday profit per day = 375 * $102 = $38,250

Now that we know the profit per day on a weekday and weekend, we can calculate the profit per week, remembering to subtract fixed costs.

Profit per week = (2 * $33,750) + (5 * $38,250) − (7 * $5,750) = $218,500

Profit per year = $218,500 * 52 = $11,362,000.

Profit over three years = 3 * $11,362,000 = $34,086,000

For the purpose of calculating ROI, we can round this number down to 34M to see if we will reach the target ROI of 20%.

ROI = (34M − 20M) / 20M = 70%

Our client should make the investment because the ROI is roughly 70%.

Practice Problem #50

Your client is a real estate development corporation that is looking to build an apartment complex on a vacant lot near a university in Cambridge, Massachusetts.

How much does your client need to charge in rent per apartment per month if they are looking to break even within 3 years?

Here is some information on the apartment complex:

- The vacant lot is a square, measuring 200 ft on one side
- The cost of purchasing the vacant lot is $100 per sq. ft.

- Regulations require that no more than 80% of the lot can be covered with buildings (e.g., there needs to be space for grass, sidewalks)

- Building construction costs are $50 per sq. ft.

- The lot is zoned for buildings up to 3 stories tall

- No apartments are allowed in the basement (below ground level)

- Utilities cost $5,000 per month

- Insurance costs $2,500 per month

- Labor costs $40,000 per full-time employee per year

- Full-time employees include: 1 custodian, 1 rental office staff, 1 security guard

- The highest paying customers prefer apartment buildings that have at least 20% of the apartment building dedicated to amenities (e.g., common areas, gym, pool)

- Market research estimates an 80% occupancy rate per year

- Apartments that are 512 sq. ft. in size would provide the most profit

Solution to #50

Let's calculate the different one-time costs:

- Land: 200 * 200 * $100 = $4M

- Building construction: 200 * 200 * 0.8 * 3 * $50 = $4.8M

Let's calculate the other costs over a 3-year period:

- Utilities: $5,000 * 12 * 3 = $180K
- Insurance: $2,500 * 12 * 3 = $90K
- Labor: 3 * $40,000 * 3 = $360K

Total costs over 3 years = $4.8M + $180K + $90K + $460K = $9.43M

Next, let's calculate how many apartments there will be.

Total apartment sq. ft. = 200 * 200 * 0.8 * 0.8 * 3 = 76,800

Number of apartments = 76,800 / 512 = 150

Occupied apartments = 150 * 0.8 = 120

Let x = rent per month

Revenue over 3 years = 120 * 12 * 3 * x = $4,320x

Finally, we can set revenue equal to costs to solve for the rent.

$4,320x = $9.43M

x = $2,183 per month (rounded)

Rent needs to be at least $2,183 per month for each apartment.

19. Next Steps

Final Thoughts

Congratulations on making it to the final chapter!

Throughout this book, you've:

- Learned or reviewed all of the fundamental math concepts, formulas, and calculations that show up in case interviews

- Completed practice problems that reinforced the math fundamentals you've learned

- Learned techniques for improving speed, accuracy, and confidence when doing case math

Remember that case math is a skill. Like any skill, it improves with practice. You don't need to be a math genius to do well.

All you need is a solid understanding of key math concepts, smart strategies for approaching problems, and the confidence to do math out loud and under pressure.

Try to spend 30 minutes a day practicing. This can include:

- Practicing full-length case interviews with a partner
- Working through full-length case interviews by yourself
- Doing math drills to improve your speed and accuracy
- Reviewing formulas to improve confidence

Keep practicing, keep learning, and stay positive. When your interview day comes, you'll knock it out of the park.

I'd Love to Hear From You

If you found this book helpful, I'd be incredibly grateful if you left a quick review on Amazon. It only takes about 30 seconds and it makes a huge difference in supporting me as an independent author.

Click the link below to leave a review:

https://www.amazon.com/review/create-review?asin=B0FCP11H6Q

Or simply scan this QR code with your phone:

I read every single review and yours would truly mean a lot.

Next Steps

Case Interviews

Case interview math is just one piece of the puzzle. To ace your case interviews and land consulting offers, you'll need to nail every single part of the case interview.

How comfortable and confident do you feel about:

- Developing structured and tailored frameworks

- Answering qualitative questions that assess your business acumen and brainstorming creativity

- Proactively leading the direction of a case interview

- Delivering a clear and compelling recommendation

Learn case interviews in as little as 7 days while saving yourself 100+ hours of prep time through our comprehensive case interview course:

https://www.hackingthecaseinterview.com/courses/consulting

Some of our students have passed their first-round interviews at McKinsey, BCG, and Bain with just a week of preparation.

Consulting Behavioral and Fit Interviews

Additionally, remember that case interviews are not the only thing that show up in consulting interviews. Every consulting firm will ask you behavioral and fit interview questions.

Are you prepared to answer interview questions such as:

- Tell me about yourself

- What makes you interested in consulting?

- Why do you want to work at this firm?

- What's your greatest weakness?

- Tell me about a time when you resolved conflict in a team

- Why should we hire you?

If you want to be prepared for 98% of behavioral and fit questions in just a few hours, check out our behavioral interview course. We'll teach you exactly how to draft answers that will impress your interviewer.

https://www.hackingthecaseinterview.com/courses/consulting-behavioral-and-fit-interview-course

Consulting Resume and Cover Letter

Lastly, don't expect to get any consulting interviews if you have a poorly written resume.

Breaking into consulting is extremely competitive. You need an outstanding resume that is tailored and optimized for consulting to help you stand out from the crowd and land interviews.

If you need professional help crafting the perfect consulting resume, I'd love to work with you. Transform your resume into one that will get you multiple interviews.

https://www.hackingthecaseinterview.com/courses/consulting-resume-review-and-editing

20. About the Author

Taylor Warfield

Taylor Warfield is a former Manager and interviewer at Bain & Company, one of the top management consulting firms in the world. He is the author of several best-selling books, including:

- Hacking the Case Interview

- The Ultimate Case Interview Workbook

- Hacking the PM Interview

- How to Write a Resume That Doesn't Suck

He is the founder of HackingTheCaseInterview.com and has a YouTube channel with millions of views.

His books, online courses, and coaching have helped thousands of students and working professionals land job offers at top-tier consulting firms including McKinsey, BCG, Bain, LEK, Oliver Wyman, Strategy&, and EY-Parthenon.

www.ingramcontent.com/pod-product-compliance
Lightning Source LLC
Chambersburg PA
CBHW070638160426
43194CB00009B/1492